Preparing for Career Success Student Activity Book

Third Edition

Jerry Ryan

Roberta Ryan

jist Works
America's Career Publisher

Preparing for Career Success Student Activity Book, Third Edition
© 2005 by Jerry Ryan and Roberta Ryan
Published by JIST Works, an imprint of JIST Publishing
7321 Shadeland Station, Suite 200
Indianapolis, IN 46256-3923
Phone: 800-648-JIST   Fax: 877-454-7839
E-mail: info@jist.com   Web site: www.jist.com

Note to Instructors

This student workbook is part of the *Preparing for Career Success* package. *Preparing for Career Success,* Third Edition (ISBN: 978-1-59357-207-5), is the student textbook. *Preparing for Career Success Teacher's Wraparound Edition,* Third Edition (ISBN: 978-1-59357-208-2), contains enrichment ideas, discussion topics, and answers to the chapter review questions in the student textbook. *Preparing for Career Success Instructor's CD-ROM,* Third Edition (ISBN: 978-1-59357-210-5), provides worksheets, tests and quizzes, and additional resource materials. *Preparing for Career Success Student Interest Inventory,* Third Edition (ISBN: 978-1-59357-212-9), is an assessment that helps students correlate their interests with career clusters. *Preparing for Career Success ExamView® Test Generator CD-ROM,* Third Edition (ISBN: 978-1-59357-211-2), provides instructors with a variety of types of test questions to assess student performance.

Visit www.jist.com for more information on JIST, free job search tips, tables of contents and sample pages, and ordering instructions on our many products!

Quantity discounts are available for JIST books. Have future editions of JIST books automatically delivered to you on publication through our convenient standing order program. Please call our Sales Department at 800-648-JIST for a free catalog and more information.

Acquisitions Editor: Barb Terry
Development Editor: Heather Stith
Copy Editors: Linda Seifert, Nancy Sixsmith
Cover Designer: Honeymoon Image & Design, Inc.
Interior Designer: Marie Kristine Parial-Leonardo
Interior Layout: Aleata Howard
Proofreader: Jeanne Clark

Printed in the United States of America
2 3 4 5 6 7 8 9   11 10 09 08 07

ISBN 978-1-59357-209-9

About *Preparing for Career Success Student Activity Book*

Together with the *Preparing for Career Success* student textbook, the material in the *Preparing for Career Success Student Activity Book* addresses issues that are important as you prepare for the world of work. From completing a tax form to planning a weekly menu, you have the opportunity to practice important life skills as you think about the career and life issues you face as a young adult.

Each chapter ends with a "Finding the Right Words" activity and a "Checking Your Location" activity. The "Finding the Right Words" activities include word searches, word scrambles, fill-in-the-blanks, and essays designed to help you review the vocabulary presented in the textbook. The "Checking Your Location" activities are a series of true/false questions that test your knowledge of chapter material. Put this information to use as you plan for a successful life and career!

Table of Contents

Unit 4: Living on Your Own

Chapter 17: Managing Your Income **141**

Chapter 18: Being a Wise Consumer **155**

Chapter 19: Achieving Wellness **169**

Preparing for Life's Many Tasks

Chapter 1

When Your Cause Is Just

The identity stage is a time for being true to a personal set of values and being loyal to self, friends, and causes. Young adults have attached their loyalty to causes for many generations, and each generation faces unique political, social, and economic problems. Review the following list of causes and the years when each cause was very popular. The causes listed are major concerns for many individuals and organizations.

Cause	Popular Years
Worker's rights (unionism)	1920s–1930s
Democracy vs. fascism	1940–1945
Democracy vs. communism	1946–1960s
Civil rights of minorities	1950s–1970s
The natural environment	1960s–present
Nuclear weapons	1950s–present
Alcohol and drug abuse	1970s–present
Gender equity (the women's movement)	1980s–present
The war in Iraq and terrorism	2000–present

1. Which cause on the list would you support most? Explain your reasons for supporting this cause.

   _____

   _____

2. What effect would your support for this particular cause have on your relationships with family and friends?

   Family: _____

   Friends: _____

3. Which cause on the list would you support least? Explain your reasons for not supporting this cause.

   _____

   _____

4. What effect would your lack of support for this particular cause have on your relationships with family and friends?

   Family: _____

   Friends: _____

5. Can you think of a cause you would add to this list? If so, write it here:_____

Why is this cause important?_____

6. Several of the causes listed in this activity may have a positive or negative influence on your future career. Select the three causes you think will influence your career success the most. Explain the influence you expect each cause would have.

Cause: _____

Influence: _____

_____

Cause: _____

Influence: _____

_____

Cause: _____

Influence: _____

_____

Interview a worker who is at least 40 years old, asking the following questions. Write down his or her responses in the space provided.

1. Which cause listed in this activity was most important to you when you were between the ages of 17 and 24?

_____

2. How did this cause influence your education, training, or career?

_____

_____

3. How did this cause influence your lifestyle?

_____

4. What influences in your life were the sources of your loyalty to this cause?

_____

5. Now that you are older and have gained more life experience, which cause listed in this activity would you consider to be most important? Why?

_____

_____

6. Which cause do you think will have the most influence on the future career success of new workers? Why?

_____

_____

7. What advice would you offer teenagers concerning their involvement with the causes listed in this activity?

_____

_____

Name_____ Class_____ Date_____

How Would You Handle the Situation?

People react differently to life situations. Imagine that you are having dinner with a good friend in a very expensive restaurant. Suddenly, the waiter drops a dish, and a small amount of yellow sauce is splattered on the sleeve of your new jacket. In each of the following, circle the response (a, b, or c) that is closest to the response you would probably make.

1. How would you feel?

   a. Nervous or apologetic

   b. Confident that you can clean your sleeve

   c. Angry

2. What would you think?

   a. I should have pulled my sleeve out of the way.

   b. We all make mistakes, but the waiter is responsible for this situation.

   c. The waiter is incompetent. He should be reprimanded by the manager.

3. What would you say?

   a. You wouldn't say anything.

   b. "You spilled some sauce on my jacket. Please bring me some club soda so I can clean it before it stains."

   c. "This situation is inexcusable. I want to speak with the manager."

4. What would be the tone of your voice?

   a. Soft

   b. Medium

   c. Loud

5. How would you act?

   a. Avoid eye contact with the waiter or quietly leave the table

   b. Maintain eye contact with the waiter and probably remain seated

   c. Stand up to face the waiter

6. How would you expect the waiter to act toward you?

   a. Apologetic and regretful

   b. Responsible and sincere

   c. Disrespectful and aloof

Results

You have expressed six personal behaviors in this activity. Total your six responses:

    Total *a* responses: _____ (Submissive behaviors)

    Total *b* responses: _____ (Assertive behaviors)

    Total *c* responses: _____ (Aggressive behaviors)

1. Which type of behavior did you express most? _____

   Describe a situation you experienced during the past six months in which you expressed this type of behavior.

   _____

   _____

   _____

   _____

2. Are you pleased with the behavior you expressed in this situation? If so, why? If not, what behavior would you have liked to express?

   _____

   _____

   _____

   _____

3. Describe a situation in which someone was unfair to you.

   _____

   _____

   _____

   _____

   Was this person's behavior submissive, assertive, or aggressive?_____

4. Describe a situation in which someone was fair but firm with you.

   _____

   _____

   _____

   _____

   Was this person's behavior submissive, assertive, or aggressive?_____

Planning for Success

List several events and activities you have been involved in during the past six months. Examples include a class you are taking, a job you're doing, a party you attended, or a trip you took.

_____

_____

_____

_____

1. Which activities on your list did you help plan?

_____

_____

2. Which planned activity was most successful?

_____

3. Which parts of the plan were responsible for the successful outcome?

_____

_____

4. If you were planning a similar activity, what would you do differently?

_____

_____

5. Which activities on your list were unplanned?

_____

_____

6. Which unplanned activity was least successful?

_____

7. How would planning have improved the outcome?

_____

_____

8. What is one future event or activity that will influence your career success?

_____

9. Are you satisfied with the plans you have made for this event or activity? If so, why? If not, why not?

_____

_____

_____

Developing Skills for the School-to-Work Transition

Whether you are in a tech-prep, traditional college prep, vocational, or work-study program, the skills you learn in high school will determine your level of entry into the world of work or your level of preparation for additional education and training beyond high school.

1. What is the highest level mathematics course you have completed?

_____

List two occupations you would be prepared to enter with this level of mathematics skill.

_____   _____

2. What is the highest level mathematics course you plan to complete during high school or college?

_____

List two occupations you would be prepared to enter with this level of mathematics skill.

_____   _____

3. What is the highest level English course you have completed?

_____

List two occupations you would be prepared to enter with this level of English skill.

_____   _____

4. What is the highest level English course you plan to complete during high school or college?

_____

List two occupations you would be prepared to enter with this level of English skill.

_____   _____

5. When you think of your future career, what are the two most important skills you will need?

_____   _____

6. Where do you expect to learn each of these skills?

_____

Finding the Right Words

Chapter 1 of your textbook contains numerous terms that employers and workers use. Recognizing and understanding these terms will help you make the important career decisions you will soon face. Unscramble the terms in column B, and match them with the definitions in column A. (Some terms may contain two words.)

Column A	Column B
Example: _a_ the paid and unpaid work you do during your lifetime	a. _____ career _____ rareec
1. ___ being paid as much as co-workers in the same occupation	b. _____ fels-petnocc
2. ___ apologetic, indifferent, passive	c. _____ raveyit
3. ___ the amount of goods and services you buy with your income	d. _____ leady facatgrinioit
4. ___ how people view their own skills, interests, and competence level	e. _____ isgreasevg
5. ___ dull and tedious labor	f. _____ quale apy
6. ___ personal connections people develop with others	g. _____ restsavei
7. ___ a periodic change in the task, pace, or location of the work	h. _____ livetear risagenn
8. ___ domineering, relentless, quarrelsome	i. _____ numha natorieslipsh
9. ___ to postpone acquiring certain things	j. _____ rugreddy
10. ___ goods and services you can buy with your earnings compared to your neighbor's earnings	k. _____ lostbeau ringsane
11. ___ persistent, understanding, cooperative	l. _____ busvisisem

Checking Your Location

For each of the following statements, write **F** if the statement is more false than true. Write **T** if the statement is more true than false.

____ **1.** As you grow older, the world of fantasy gives way to the real world.

____ **2.** Most teenagers dislike being placed in adult roles.

____ **3.** Developing a career plan now will help you achieve a higher level of success later in life.

____ **4.** Your parents and teachers are responsible for your career satisfaction.

____ **5.** Submissive people frequently have problems with everyday life situations because of their failure to communicate their beliefs honestly.

____ **6.** Assertive people express their feelings and values openly and honestly.

____ **7.** Psychological and social concerns are unimportant to a person who works with tools.

____ **8.** Work that is valued by the worker can be paid or unpaid.

____ **9.** Several things that are far more important than the size of your paycheck will determine your future lifestyle.

____ **10.** Regardless of their age, sex, or race, people expect to be paid as much as their co-workers.

____ **11.** Job security is largely determined by the size of the company you work for.

____ **12.** Human relationships are a very important work value for some people.

____ **13.** For some workers, having a variety of work tasks is directly related to job satisfaction.

____ **14.** The basic skills of reading, writing, and mathematics are related to success on the job.

____ **15.** Failure on the job may cause feelings of role confusion, anger, depression, and incompetence.

On a separate sheet of paper, rewrite the statements you marked false and make them true. Include the number of each statement you write.

Knowing Yourself: Interests and Aptitudes Chapter 2

What Makes You Different?

In Chapter 2 of your textbook, you learned about the interaction of your heredity, culture, environment, and life experiences. You learned how this interaction creates the unique traits and characteristics that are you. Increasing your level of self-understanding in each of these areas will help you gain further control over your life goals and personal choices as you prepare for career success.

Heredity

1. Think about your family members (living or dead). Which family member is (or was) most similar to you?

   Name: _____

   Relationship: _____

2. What behaviors, talents, or physical features did you inherit from this person? Consider your size and temperament and traits such as musical or mechanical skills.

   _____

   _____

3. How are you different from the person you selected?

   _____

   _____

Life Experiences

1. Describe two or more life experiences of yours that are different from the life experiences of the family member you selected.

   _____

   _____

2. How did the life experiences you described influence the person you are?

   _____

   _____

   _____

3. Describe two or more life experiences of yours that are similar to the life experiences of the family member you selected.

_____

_____

_____

4. How did the life experiences you described influence the family member you selected?

_____

_____

_____

Culture

Think about the culture in which you live. Think about the way of life of the people with whom you interact. What important belief have you learned and accepted from the people

In your home? _____

_____

In your school? _____

_____

In your house of worship? _____

_____

In your neighborhood? _____

_____

Environment

Your surroundings influence your beliefs, attitudes, and lifestyle choices. Describe the environment in which you live (urban or rural, climate, geographic features):

_____

_____

_____

How has your environment influenced your beliefs, attitudes, or lifestyle choices?

_____

_____

_____

_____

_____

Name_____ Class_____ Date_____

Workers in Your Family Tree

Ask a parent, guardian, family friend, or agency worker to help you obtain information for the following chart.

Relationship	First and Last Name of Relative	Where Relative Lived	Occupation(s) of Relative	Personal Qualities
Maternal grandmother				
Maternal grandfather				
Paternal grandmother				
Paternal grandfather				
Great-grandmother				
Great-grandfather				

Use the information from this chart to answer the following questions. Select any three of the workers listed in your family tree.

1. Has this relative's occupation changed greatly or disappeared? Explain.

Name of relative:_____

Answer:_____

Name of relative:_____

Answer:_____

Name of relative:_____

Answer:_____

2. Have the education and training requirements for this occupation changed? Explain.

Name of relative:_____

Answer:_____

Name of relative:_____

Answer:_____

Name of relative:_____

Answer:_____

3. Imagine that you lived during the time of your great-grandparents. What occupation would you probably have?

_____

4. Would you have more or less freedom to choose your occupation than you do now? Explain your answer.

_____

_____

Self-Concept

Self is the part of your experience that you regard as essentially you. It is how you see yourself in the past, present, and future. Your attitude toward yourself determines whether you view yourself with pride or shame, as worthy or unworthy. It affects the attitude you have toward others.

1. What kinds of things could you do during your elementary school years?

_____

_____

_____

2. What difficulties did you have when you were younger?

_____

_____

3. What or who is most important in your past?

_____

4. How do you see yourself now? Use at least 50 words to describe yourself.

_____

_____

_____

_____

_____

_____

5. What commonalities in your past and present describe you?

_____

_____

_____

6. What do you want to do with your life in the next 50 years?

_____

_____

_____

_____

_____

Self-Esteem

Many employers link an employee's effectiveness in the workplace directly to positive self-esteem and successful personal management. Employees with positive self-esteem recognize their current skill level on the job; are aware of their impact on others; understand their emotions and cope well with stress, change, and criticism; deal with their limitations by seeking and applying new information to solve problems; and take pride in their work. Evaluate yourself in terms of some of these points as they relate to your "job" as a student.

1. Do you recognize your current skill level in each of your school subjects? Explain your answer.

_____

_____

_____

2. Are you aware of your impact on others? Give an example.

_____

_____

_____

3. Do you understand your emotions and cope well with stress, change, and criticism? Give an example.

_____

_____

_____

4. Do you deal with your limitations by seeking and applying new information to solve problems? Give an example.

_____

_____

_____

5. Do you take pride in your school work? Give an example.

_____

_____

_____

Positive self-esteem expresses an attitude of approval and positive evaluation. One indication of positive self-esteem is the number of positive statements a person makes about self or others. People with low self-esteem tend to make many negative comments about their own behavior or that of others.

1. How many positive (yes) statements did you make in this activity? _____

2. How many negative (no) statements did you make?_____

3. With which negative statement are you most dissatisfied? _____

4. What action could you take that would cause you to feel better about this situation?

_____

_____

Identifying Interests

Inventoried interests are estimates of interests based on responses to a set of questions concerning likes and dislikes. People and jobs reflect patterns of interest. The following are activities that people do. Select *all* the activities you are interested in now as well as those you would like to try. Write **L** (for Like) on the line next to the matching number in the Answers section at the end of this activity.

1. Skiing or ice skating
2. Repairing things
3. Playing chess
4. Sketching or painting
5. Visiting friends
6. Being a club officer
7. Collecting special items
8. Fishing or hunting
9. Being athletic
10. Reading science fiction
11. Reading or writing poetry
12. Going to a party
13. Expressing my viewpoints
14. Keeping a diary
15. Farming or gardening
16. Working on cars
17. Writing computer programs
18. Doing art or photography projects
19. Caring for pets
20. Being a leader

21. Working crossword puzzles
22. Jogging or hiking
23. Building or making things
24. Building models
25. Writing stories
26. Caring for plants
27. Being a referee or umpire
28. Attending worship services
29. Playing outdoor games
30. Doing physical activities
31. Building science projects
32. Singing or dancing
33. Writing to a friend
34. Being a student leader
35. Selling items for school
36. Riding a bike
37. Doing hands-on class projects
38. Using a microscope
39. Playing a musical instrument

40. Talking with friends
41. Campaigning for class officers
42. Attending club meetings
43. Boating or swimming
44. Making things in shop class
45. Reading mystery stories
46. Being in plays
47. Doing volunteer work
48. Earning awards or certificates
49. Playing spelling games
50. Learning about the outdoors
51. Learning about machines
   about science
   about art or music
   child care
   politics
   work

1. ___	2. ___	3. ___				
8. ___	9. ___	10. ___				
15. ___	16. ___	17. ___				
22. ___	23. ___	24. ___	25. ___			___
29. ___	30. ___	31. ___	32. ___			5. ___
36. ___	37. ___	38. ___	39. ___			42. ___
43. ___	44. ___	45. ___	46. ___			49. ___
50. ___	51. ___	52. ___	53. ___	54. ___	___	56. ___

Total → ☐ 1 ☐ 2 ☐ 3 ☐ 4 ☐ 5 ☐ 6 ☐ 7

Total the number of **L**s in each column. Enter each score in the correct box. You will use these totals in the "Identifying Your Personal Orientations" worksheet in Chapter 4.

Skills—Now and for Tomorrow

Skills are the competencies you have developed through education, training, or life experience. All jobs require specific skills. When you have the ability to perform a task well, you are a skilled worker.

Review the following list, and select *all* the skills you have now or plan to develop in the future. Write an S (for *Skill*) on the line next to the matching number in the Answers section at the end of this activity.

1. Planting, cultivating, or harvesting a garden
2. Building things with tools
3. Understanding technical information
4. Playing, writing, or performing music
5. Taking care of people or animals
6. Being a leader
7. Keeping track of numbers, systems, people, or records
8. Developing outdoor survival skills
9. Repairing or u___ ical things
10. Observing, experime___ tific info___
11. Findin___ thing___
12. Usi___ p___
13. ___

15. Developing outdoor camping skills
16. Using tools and drawings to repair things
17. Solving math or science problems
18. Performing in dramas or dance
19. Planning social activities for groups of people
20. Organizing students for an activity
21. Keeping neat and accurate records
___ Observing behavior pat___ of birds
___ clothes___
___ ite
___ ith
___ aker
___ work

29. Developing fishing or hunting skills
30. Driving or operating a vehicle
31. Figuring out problems
32. Visualizing objects and creating drawings
33. Explaining ideas to people
34. Setting and reaching goals
35. Keeping accurate records
36. Doing yard work
37. Operating machinery or equipment
38. Understanding good chess moves and strategy games
39. Expressing feelings or ideas through art, music, or writing
40. Teaching or instructing people
41. Convincing people to do things your way
42. Knowing and following correct rules and procedures

[Handwritten notes overlaid on page: "Pick 10 Personality traits you think best describe" / "Sully" / "Mike" / "Waternoose" / "Randall" / "Skills , Interests"]

Answers

1. ___			4. ___	5. ___	6. ___	7. ___
8. ___	9. ___		11. ___	12. ___	13. ___	14. ___
15. ___	16. ___		18. ___	19. ___	20. ___	21. ___
22. ___	23. ___	24. ___	25. ___	26. ___	27. ___	28. ___
29. ___	30. ___	31. ___	32. ___	33. ___	34. ___	35. ___
36. ___	37. ___	38. ___	39. ___	40. ___	41. ___	42. ___
□ 1	□ 2	□ 3	□ 4	□ 5	□ 6	□ 7

[Handwritten: "Total → 7"]

Total the number of Ss in each column. Enter each score in the correct box. You will use these totals in the "Identifying Your Personal Orientations" worksheet in Chapter 4.

Data, People, or Things?

The following is a list of job activities. Place a check mark in front of all the activities you would prefer. Some people will choose many activities, and others will choose only a few. Review the "Data, People, and Things" section (page 33) in Chapter 2 of your textbook for a complete explanation of this topic.

A	**B**	**C**
____ Giving professional advice to people	____ Putting new ideas and facts together	____ Understanding, fixing, changing, and operating equipment
____ Resolving conflicts	____ Deciding on the organized projects	____ Choosing and using tools to exact standards
____ Teaching or demonstrating	____ Solving problems with information	____ Operating complex equipment
____ Directing or helping others	____ Collecting, arranging, and reporting information	____ Steering, operating, and guiding machinery
____ Entertaining others	____ Using mathematics for reports	____ Using tools to move, guide, or place things
____ Influencing others' opinions or use of services or products	____ Copying numbers or words precisely	____ Starting, stopping, and watching machines
____ Making yourself understood through speech	____ Comparing likes and differences	____ Filling or emptying automatic machinery
____ Serving or assisting others		____ Moving or carrying things
____ Following verbal instructions		

1. Enter the number of check marks in list A: ____

   This number represents your *people* score.

2. Enter the number of check marks in list B: ____

   This number is your *data* score.

3. Enter the number of check marks in list C: ____

   This number is your *things* score.

4. Using your scores from this activity, determine which are most important to you: people, data, or things. (Higher numbers indicate greater importance.) If two scores are the same, determine their order of importance.

   Most important: _____

   Second most important: _____

   Least important: _____

5. What skills do you need to acquire to be eligible for a job you would enjoy in the category you chose as "most important"?

   _____

   _____

Finding the Right Words

Chapter 2 of your textbook contains numerous terms that employers and workers use. Recognizing and understanding these terms will help you make the important career decisions you will soon face. Unscramble the terms in column B, and match them with the definitions in column A. (Some terms may contain more than one word.)

Column A	Column B
Example: _a_ your potential for success in a certain activity	a. ____aptitude____ tiadeptu
1. ____ your sense of morality	b. _____ cavoatino
2. ____ your judgment about your level of competence	c. _____ theeridy
3. ____ tasks involving machines	d. _____ sitenret vussery
4. ____ the combination of all of your psychological parts	e. _____ relucut
5. ____ the way you typically act, feel, and think	f. _____ resulie miet
6. ____ preferences for certain topics and activities	g. _____ revinmonten
7. ____ tasks involving personal relationships	h. _____ ibaitly
8. ____ what you think of as you	i. _____ rogwink hitw tada
9. ____ free time	j. _____ syonerpalit
10. ____ an activity that provides personal satisfaction	k. _____ lefs-semete
11. ____ people who set behavior standards for you	l. _____ stenister
12. ____ how well you perform certain tasks	m. _____ hactecrar
13. ____ tests used to measure preferences	n. _____ creneeref suprog *reference groups*
14. ____ tasks involving information	o. _____ kogrinw ihwt lopeep
15. ____ your surroundings	p. _____ petemmanter
16. ____ characteristics being passed from parent to child	q. _____ rokwgin thiw stingh
17. ____ the way of life in the society in which you live	r. _____ fels

Checking Your Location

For each of the following statements, write **F** if the statement is more false than true. Write **T** if the statement is more true than false.

_____ **1.** From the day you were born, your environment has influenced you; in turn, you have influenced your environment.

_____ **2.** Physical features, intelligence, reflexes, and temperament are part of your heredity.

_____ **3.** Your attitude toward education and training is not affected by your culture.

_____ **4.** Most psychologists believe that personality is formed late in childhood.

_____ **5.** A person can have high interest but low ability in certain areas, and vice versa.

_____ **6.** Personality traits change a great deal as you get older, so the results of accurate testing are of very little use over a long period of time.

_____ **7.** Self-concept can be thought of as your attitude toward your personality.

_____ **8.** It is wise to compare interests, abilities, temperament, and character with the worker traits of an occupation before deciding to acquire the education and training needed to enter the occupation.

_____ **9.** Your self-concept was formed at birth.

_____ **10.** A person with a high level of self-esteem feels competent, of value to society, in control of most life events, important to other people, and useful.

_____ **11.** Your interests are related to only one occupation.

_____ **12.** People usually possess one or more aptitudes that haven't been developed to a high level of skill.

_____ **13.** Once you have identified your strong aptitudes, it is important to use your potential and learn specific career skills.

_____ **14.** Every occupation requires workers to spend some of their time performing tasks working with data, people, and things.

_____ **15.** Leisure-time pursuits are poor ways to identify possible interests in certain career areas.

On a separate sheet of paper, rewrite the statements you marked false and make them true. Include the number of each statement you rewrite.

Knowing Yourself: Values and Goals

Chapter **3**

Examining Your Work Values

When you think about work and careers, how do you decide what is right or wrong, wise or foolish? Six groups of work values are listed below. Draw circles around the numbers of the three values in each group that are most important to you. You may not place a high value on any of the work values listed—but select three from each group that you value most. Write **M** (for *most important to me*) on the appropriate line in the Answers section at the end of this activity.

Group 1
1. Working in the outdoors
2. Working with tools
3. Working with numbers or facts
4. Developing new procedures
5. Showing concern for people
6. Influencing people
7. Having secure work during recessions

Group 2
8. Working with plants or animals
9. Using mechanical skills
10. Investigating information or data
11. Creating new products or services
12. Having good relations with coworkers
13. Leading other workers to achieve goals
14. Working with clearly defined tasks

Group 3
15. Preserving the natural environment
16. Using high-quality tools and machines
17. Analyzing problems with work
18. Expressing feelings through work
19. Helping coworkers be successful
20. Having the respect of other workers
21. Working for a well-organized employer

Group 4
22. Doing work involving nature
23. Using my hands
24. Solving problems
25. Using my imagination
26. Helping people
27. Leading others
28. Checking accuracy

Group 5
29. Working in a natural setting
30. Keeping machinery working well
31. Working with scientific skills
32. Making my own work decisions
33. Making fellow workers happy
34. Being in charge of projects
35. Having a secure insurance plan

Group 6
36. Working with natural resources
37. Repairing mechanical devices
38. Understanding work facts
39. Creating new methods of working
40. Teaching job skills to others
41. Making decisions about the work
42. Having ethical, moral coworkers

Answers

1. ___	2. ___	3. ___	4. ___	5. ___	6. ___	7. ___
8. ___	9. ___	10. ___	11. ___	12. ___	13. ___	14. ___
15. ___	16. ___	17. ___	18. ___	19. ___	20. ___	21. ___
22. ___	23. ___	24. ___	25. ___	26. ___	27. ___	28. ___
29. ___	30. ___	31. ___	32. ___	33. ___	34. ___	35. ___
36. ___	37. ___	38. ___	39. ___	40. ___	41. ___	42. ___
☐	☐	☐	☐	☐	☐	☐
1	2	3	4	5	6	7

Total the number of **M**s in each column. Enter each score in the correct box. You will use these totals in the "Identifying Your Personal Orientations" worksheet in Chapter 4.

What's Most Important?

When you think about career goals, do you sometimes feel confused or lost? If this happens, use your values for a compass, and follow their direction. Use the following rating scale to express the importance you place on the career goals listed in columns I and II. Keep in mind that there is no right or wrong answer. Then answer the questions about your ratings.

Rating Scale: 1 = Very important to me; 2 = Somewhat important to me; 3 = Of average importance to me; 4 = Not very important to me; 5 = Unimportant to me.

Column I

____ Helping people

____ Having the respect of coworkers

____ Having a very secure job

____ Having a job that is challenging

____ Having a job I enjoy

____ Spending my life in one community

____ Improving the life of others

____ Making decisions about my work

Column II

____ Earning a large amount of money

____ Owning an entertainment system

____ Affording expensive vacations

____ Owning a first-class home

____ Affording very nice clothes

____ Owning a new automobile

____ Dining in nice restaurants

____ Buying nice things for my family

1. Which three career goals are the most important to you? _____

   _____

   _____

2. Which three career goals are least important to you? _____

   _____

   _____

3. Column I lists nonmaterialistic career goals. Total the rating points you recorded for the career goals in Column I. Write the total here: ____

4. Column II lists materialistic career goals. Total the rating points you recorded for the career goals in column II. Write the total here: ____

5. Do your total scores for Column I and Column II indicate that you are more inclined toward materialistic or nonmaterialistic career goals? (Higher scores indicate a stronger inclination.)

   _____

6. Review the three career goals you listed as most important in question 2. Next, review the three career goals you listed as least important in question 3. Do your selections indicate that you are more inclined toward materialistic or nonmaterialistic career goals?

   _____

Review "Section 2: Goals," in Chapter 3 of your textbook for more information.

Name_____ **Class**_____ **Date**_____

The Time Is Now!

A wristwatch, alarm clock, or calendar is a handy tool if you are measuring the passage of time. Tools, machines, instruments, books, paper, and pens are better tools if you are making wise use of the present. Once you establish an educational or occupational goal, you will need to make wise use of these tools every day.

1. How did you spend your waking hours yesterday? List your two most time-consuming accomplishments and the amount of time you spent on each.

Accomplishment:_____ Time spent:_____

Accomplishment:_____ Time spent:_____

Will either of your accomplishments help you achieve an educational or occupational goal? If so, describe how. If no, describe a different accomplishment that would have made wiser use of your time.

_____

_____

2. List one or more activities that you currently accomplish at least three times a week as preparation for an educational occupational goal. Circle the activity that you consider to be most important.

_____

_____

When you are involved with the activity you circled, do you remove or avoid distractions? If so, what distractions, and how? If not, why not?

_____

_____

How much time do you allow for this activity? _____

Is this enough time? If so, how are you measuring your success? If not, how could you readjust your schedule to acquire more time?

_____

_____

3. In each of the following pairs of choices, circle the choice that is closest to your daily use of time:

A. I live for today.   B. I plan for tomorrow.

A. I am frequently late.   B. I am usually on time.

A. I worry about things I can't change.   B. I don't let my fears get in my way.

A. I make excuses for not completing my work. B. My work is usually completed on time.

How many A responses did you circle?____ How many B responses?____

The A responses are less mature; the B responses are more mature.

Your Attitude Is Showing

Your attitude is the way you think about things and act toward others. Consider the following situation: You are working the evening shift on a Friday. Saturday is your scheduled day off, and you plan to attend a friend's birthday party. One of your coworkers called in sick with the flu. Because of his absence, your entire team must work faster. Your supervisor is helping the team as much as possible, but she has work tasks of her own to complete. Yesterday, the employee who called in sick told you he was invited to go away for the weekend, but he was scheduled to work. You question whether he really is ill. During your first break, your supervisor cancels your day off and tells you that she will need you to work Saturday evening.

1. How would you react to this situation? List four of your immediate feelings.

_____ _____ _____ _____

2. List three things you would probably say to your supervisor or another person.

_____

_____

_____

3. List three things you would do as a result of this situation.

_____

_____

_____

Carefully consider each of your 10 responses to this situation. Determine whether each response is more positive (constructive or helpful) or more negative (uncooperative). Place a plus sign (+) next to each positive response and a minus sign (−) next to each negative response.

How many of your responses were positive? ____

Use the following table to identify the type of attitude you displayed in this particular situation.

Number of Positive Responses	Type of Attitude Displayed
1–3	Strong negative attitude
4	Weak negative attitude
5	Weak attitude
6	Weak positive attitude
7–10	Strong positive attitude

What probable influence would your 10 responses have on your future promotions and pay increases?

_____

If you had waited for one hour before you said anything to your supervisor or another person, how might the outcome of this situation been different?

_____

Name_____ **Class**_____ **Date**_____

Lifestyle Options

The demands and rewards of your future occupation will place limits on certain lifestyle options and will open the door to others.

Occupational Choice

1. Write the name of an occupation you are seriously considering for your future career.

   _____

2. What are the education and training requirements for this occupation?

   _____

3. What are the average annual earnings for this occupation? $_____

Lifestyle Options

1. What type of vehicle do you expect to own 10 years from now? _____

2. What is the present market value of this type of vehicle? $_____

3. Is this lifestyle option consistent with your occupational choice? Provide facts to support your answer. _____

4. What type of home do you expect to live in 10 years from now? _____

5. What is the present market value or annual lease or rental payment for this type of home?
   $_____

6. Is this lifestyle option consistent with your occupational choice? Provide facts to support your answer.

   _____

   _____

7. Name two leisure-time activities you expect to be involved in 10 years from now.

   _____

8. How many hours per week will you spend participating in these leisure activities? _____

9. What hours of the day, evening, or weekend will you be involved in these leisure activities?

   _____

10. What will be the monthly cost of your activities? $_____

11. Is this lifestyle option consistent with your occupational choice? Provide facts to support your answer.

    _____

    _____

Take Note: Accurate salary and training information for this activity is available in the *Occupational Outlook Handbook.* See your school counselor or librarian.

Finding the Right Words

Chapter 3 of your textbook contains numerous terms that employers and workers use. Recognizing and understanding these terms will help you make the important career decisions you will soon face. Unscramble the terms in column B, and match them with the definitions in column A. (Some terms may contain two words.)

Column A	Column B
Example: __a__ cherished ideas and beliefs	a. _____ values
1. ___ opinions formed beforehand	b. _____ saveul
2. ___ trial		
3. ___ an attitude that refuses to change	laterismoantinic
	c. _____
4. ___ how you think about things and act toward others	devinecorpec feelsbi
	d. _____
5. ___ a goal that provides inner satisfaction	tudateit
	e. _____
6. ___ the people you frequently come in contact with	avetitent
	f. _____
7. ___ an aim or objective	redjupice
	g. _____
8. ___ the way you live	bitangle
	h. _____
9. ___ parts	itisrealc
	i. _____
10. ___ obtainable	mite nile
	j. _____
11. ___ schedule	alog
	k. _____
12. ___ anything you can touch	moonentscp
	l. _____
	filetyle
	m. _____
	coalis removeitnnn

Checking Your Location

For each of the following statements, write **F** if the statement is more false than true. Write **T** if the statement is more true than false.

_____ **1.** Values are moral truths that guide your life.

_____ **2.** Choosing an occupation that is related to your values will increase your likelihood of career success.

_____ **3.** Achieving materialistic career goals provides a great deal of inner satisfaction.

_____ **4.** Your lifestyle has nothing to do with the occupation you choose.

_____ **5.** Work adds a sense of purpose to a person's values.

_____ **6.** Setting realistic goals puts you in charge of the direction your career takes.

_____ **7.** For every short-term goal you achieve, you will need several long-term goals.

_____ **8.** Some day-to-day tasks are not interesting, but all successful workers perform some tasks they dislike.

_____ **9.** A prejudice is an attitude you have about people from a racial, religious, or ethnic background that differs from your own.

_____ **10.** Your future lifestyle will be a compromise between the lifestyle options you select and the requirements and rewards of your future occupation.

_____ **11.** Learning to make lifestyle adjustments and adapting to new and sometimes unwanted situations are necessary elements of every successful career.

_____ **12.** Achieving a goal gives you a sense of accomplishment and raises your level of self-esteem.

_____ **13.** Failing to achieve a goal will make you a better person. Failure will motivate you to try again and work harder.

_____ **14.** People with well-defined values also have high levels of self-understanding and self-esteem.

_____ **15.** Once you have a clear understanding of your values, interests, and aptitudes, it will be time to set career goals.

On a separate sheet of paper, rewrite the statements you marked false and make them true. Include the number of each statement you rewrite.

Problem Solving: Making Choices

Chapter 4

What's Your Style?

Every day, you face situations in which you must choose between two or more options. The choices you make influence the outcome of your daily activities and personal interactions. They also influence your future career and lifestyle. Five decision-making styles are described in your textbook. What's your style?

Authority: You rely on a spouse, parent, or other person.
Intuitive: You rely on values and personal feelings.
Fatalistic: You believe outcomes are predetermined and unavoidable.
Impulsive: You decide quickly before considering outcomes.
Rational: You consider the values and feelings of the decision maker, facts, and possible outcomes.

1. Which decision-making style would you use in each of the following situations? Why?

Deciding which medicine to take for an illness.

Style: _____

Reason: _____

Deciding which house of worship to attend.

Style: _____

Reason: _____

Deciding which pair of shoes to buy at a sale.

Style: _____

Reason: _____

Deciding which mathematics course to take.

Style: _____

Reason: _____

Deciding which occupation to prepare for.

Style: _____

Reason: _____

2. Which decision-making style do you use the most? _____

3. Why do you prefer this style? _____

_____

4. Describe a decision you made using this style. _____

_____

5. Which decision-making style do you use the least? _____

6. Why do you avoid using this style? _____

Identifying Your Personal Orientations

In Chapters 2 and 3 of this workbook, you completed three activities expressing personal preferences and perceptions about your interests, skills, and values. The following tabulation of your results will help you relate the preferences and perceptions you expressed toward seven groups of characteristics. Fill in the chart with the numbers from the Answers section of the listed activities.

Activity	1	2	3	4	5	6	7
Chapter 2: Identifying Interests							
Chapter 2: Skills—Now and for Tomorrow							
Chapter 3: Examining Your Work Values							
Total							

The seven categories of preferences and perceptions you have totaled in this activity correspond to the following numbered descriptions of the seven broad groups of personal characteristics called *orientations* (unique individual directions). Review the following descriptions of the seven orientations. An understanding of how important these orientations are to you will help you explore careers in the U.S. Department of Education's career clusters.

1. *Environmental:* People with this characteristic are physically active, are interested in nature, and enjoy outdoor activities.

2. *Mechanical:* People with this characteristic are physically active and like using tools, machines, or instruments to build or repair things.

3. *Scientific:* People with this characteristic like investigating information or data to help them understand ideas and the causes of events.

4. *Creative:* People with this characteristic frequently enjoy music, art, or literature. They like to use new methods and ideas.

5. *Sociable:* People with this characteristic enjoy helping people and discussing problems or situations.

6. *Persuasive:* People with this characteristic like to organize groups of people to accomplish goals. They are skilled at convincing and persuading.

7. *Structured:* People with this characteristic are skilled at organizing and categorizing information or numerical data. They prefer proven methods to new ideas.

Using the preceding descriptions and the totals from the chart, determine which orientations are most and least like you. For example, if your highest total was in the 1 column in the chart, the environmental orientation (the description numbered 1) is most like you. If your lowest total was in the 6 column, the persuasive orientation (the description numbered 6) is least like you.

1. Which two orientations are most like you? _____ _____

2. Which orientation is most unlike you? _____

Review the section "Matching Characteristics to Careers" in Chapter 4 of your textbook for more information.

Connecting to the Career Clusters

The 16 career clusters located in the appendix of your textbook follow a system used by the U.S. Department of Education. Most occupations occur to some degree in each of the 16 clusters. However, the majority of occupations within each cluster share a common work environment. Additionally, each occupation performs clearly defined job tasks. These work environments and job tasks relate to the seven occupational orientations.

The following list shows the 16 career clusters and the orientations to which they are closely related. The orientations are rated by levels of importance with 1 being the most important. As you review the list, keep in mind the orientations you identified in the preceding "Identifying Your Personal Orientations" worsksheet.

Career Cluster	Occupational Orientation(s)
Agricultural and Natural Resources	1. Environmental 2. Mechanical 3. Structured 4. Scientific
Architecture and Construction	1. Mechanical 2. Environmental 3. Scientific 4. Structured
Arts, A/V Technology, and Communication	1. Creative 2. Scientific 3. Sociable 4. Mechanical
Business and Administration	1. Structured 2. Persuasive 3. Sociable
Education and Training	1. Sociable 2. Persuasive 3. Creative 4. Scientific
Finance	1. Persuasive 2. Structured 3. Sociable
Government and Public Administration	All occupations and orientations are found in this cluster.
Health Science	1. Scientific 2. Mechanical 3. Creative 4. Sociable
Hospitality and Tourism	1. Persuasive 2. Sociable 3. Structured 4. Environmental
Human Services	1. Sociable 2. Structured 3. Persuasive
Information Technology	1. Scientific 2. Structured 3. Mechanical 4. Creative
Law and Public Safety	1. Structured 2. Persuasive 3. Sociable
Manufacturing	1. Mechanical 2. Scientific 3. Structured
Retail/Wholesale Sales and Service	1. Persuasive 2. Sociable 3. Creative 4. Mechanical
Scientific Research and Engineering	1. Scientific 2. Mechanical 3. Creative
Transportation, Distribution, and Logistics	1. Environmental 2. Structured 3. Mechanical 4. Investigative

1. Which career clusters relate to the career orientations with your two highest scores (see the "Identifying Your Personal Orientations" worsksheet)?

_____

Review occupations listed in the career clusters you identified (see appendix of your textbook). List the occupation(s) that interest you most here.

_____

2. Which career clusters relate to the career orientation with your lowest score?

_____

3. Review occupations listed in the career clusters you identified (see the appendix of your textbook). List the occupation(s) you dislike most here.

_____

Deciding What Education and Training You Need

It is important to take certain steps toward a future occupational goal while you are still a student. One of these steps is deciding what education and training you will need for the occupation you select. Review "The Rational Decision-Making Process" in Chapter 4 of your textbook before beginning this activity.

Considering a Problem

You will probably have several jobs during your lifetime. What is the title of the highest level job you expect to achieve during the next 10 years?

_____

1. Circle the level of education and training that is required for entry into the job you have selected.

   High school

   One-year technical school

   Two-year college

   Four-year college or higher

2. For the job you have selected, what will be the highest level course required in the following subject areas? (Be specific.)

   English: _____

   Mathematics: _____

   Science: _____

   An area of special training: _____

3. At the conclusion of the current school year, what will be the highest level course requirement you have successfully completed in the following subject areas? (Be specific.)

   English: _____

   Mathematics: _____

   Science: _____

   An area of special training: _____

4. To become qualified for the job you have selected, what specific courses will you need to enroll in next? (Be specific.)

   English: _____

   Mathematics: _____

   Science: _____

   An area of special training: _____

Making a Decision

1. Now you must make a decision. Do you plan to continue your education and enroll in the next level of required courses to enter the job you have selected? If so, when will you enroll?

   _____

   _____

   _____

2. List the facts you considered before you made this decision.

   _____

   _____

   _____

3. Could you have obtained additional facts before making your decision? If so, where? If not, why not?

   _____

   _____

   _____

4. Are you satisfied with your decision? If so, why? If not, why not?

   _____

   _____

   _____

5. What course of action will you follow to carry out your decision?

   _____

   _____

   _____

The Choice Is Yours

Imagine that you and two of your best friends are hiking in a large park. Write their first names here.
Friend 1: _____ Friend 2: _____

It is a sunny October day. The temperature is in the 70s, but it will drop to the 40s during the night. Friend 1 is carrying a knapsack containing two oranges, two sandwiches, a plastic rain poncho, and a box of matches. Friend 2 has a one-quart canteen of water and a liter bottle of pop. You have a wristwatch, a small pocketknife, and two candy bars. Each of you has a lightweight jacket and a hat. About four miles from the park entrance, you decide to follow an interesting trail with no directional signs. Within a few minutes your group is lost—no sign of a trail and no sound of people. Friend 2 slips on wet leaves and falls down a small hill. The result is a severely twisted ankle that might be fractured. Friend 2 is unable to walk. It is late afternoon, and Friend 1 points out a bear on a hill about a half mile away. A mountain stream is flowing nearby. It is time to make some decisions.

1. What will you do first? _____

2. How will your group select a leader? _____

3. Who will take charge? _____

4. How will the three of you work together? _____

5. What work tasks will need to be performed? Who will be responsible for each task?

Work Task	Responsible Person

6. What are the two most important decisions you have made?

_____

_____

7. How did you make these important decisions?

_____

_____

Finding the Right Words

Chapter 4 of your textbook contains numerous terms that employers and workers use. Recognizing and understanding these terms will help you make the important career decisions you will soon face. Fill in the blank spaces using the vocabulary terms to complete the following sentences.

1. When a person acts on a decision, there are always _____.

2. Qualities that make an individual unique are called _____.

3. Your unique individual direction is referred to as your _____.

4. The ability to recognize forms in space and the relationships of plane and solid objects is called

   _____.

5. Another term for decision making is_____.

6. A style of decision making that is based on personal feelings and values rather than facts is called _____.

7. Believing that whatever you decide will happen anyway is known as the _____ style of decision making.

8. The skill to examine your thoughts and feelings is called _____.

9. The word _____ means bringing others together, pacifying, or winning them over.

10. Work settings are frequently referred to as _____.

11. When you share another person's thoughts and feelings, you are _____.

12. People with a _____ orientation tend to rely on their feelings and emotions more than on information or facts.

13. People with a _____ orientation use their intellect more than their social or physical skills to solve problems.

14. People with a _____ orientation enjoy being helpful.

15. People with a _____ orientation prefer work involving machines and tools.

16. People with a _____ orientation enjoy sales and leadership roles.

17. People with a _____ orientation are frequently skilled in coding, classifying, and computing information.

Checking Your Location

For each of the following statements, write **F** if the statement is more false than true. Write **T** if the statement is more true than false.

_____ **1.** Every day, you face situations in which you must make choices.

_____ **2.** Using the authority style of decision making makes a person feel very independent.

_____ **3.** A rational style of decision making considers the feelings and values of the decision maker as well as the facts of the situation.

_____ **4.** A decision isn't a decision until something happens.

_____ **5.** The possibility of risk and failure can create feelings of confusion, conflict, and anxiety.

_____ **6.** Once a decision is made, you shouldn't change it.

_____ **7.** People with strong scientific orientation enjoy working with tools and machines. They are usually skilled at repairing mechanical devices.

_____ **8.** People with strong structured orientation solve problems using new ideas and the latest information.

_____ **9.** As you grow older and gain career experience, your skill level will increase and your career hopes and goals will change.

_____ **10.** As a responsible adult, it is very important to have an effective process for making decisions.

_____ **11.** Understanding yourself and all the facts of the situation will help you make realistic, acceptable decisions.

_____ **12.** People with a strong creative orientation like to examine the rules of the organization and how society might react before they begin a project.

_____ **13.** People with a strong mechanical orientation often develop their physical skills more fully than their human relation and verbal communication skills.

On a separate sheet of paper, rewrite the statements you marked false and make them true. Include the number of each statement you rewrite.

Researching and Understanding Career Information

Chapter **5**

The *Occupational Outlook Handbook*

Use the *Occupational Outlook Handbook (OOH)* in your school library or in your counselor's office for this activity.

1. Browse through the *OOH*'s table of contents. Notice how related occupations are grouped according to the Standard Occupational Classification System. This system is based on the type of work performed in occupations. Which of the clusters are you considering most seriously for your future occupation?

   _____

   _____

2. Read the section "How to Interpret Occupational Information Included in the *Handbook*," and describe what you will learn about in each of the following categories when you use the *OOH* to research occupations.

   Nature of the work: _____

   _____

   Working conditions: _____

   _____

   Training, other qualifications, and advancement: _____

   _____

   Job outlook:_____

   _____

   Earnings: _____

   _____

   Related occupations: _____

   _____

   Sources of additional information: _____

   _____

3. Look in the index at the back of the *OOH*. On the following line, write the name of the occupation you are most interested in pursuing for your future career and the page number where you can find information about this occupation:

   _____

Find and Use Career Information

The satisfaction you receive from your career will depend on how well your choice of an occupation meets your personal, social, and economic needs and expectations. Career information can help you discover several occupations that may meet your needs and expectations. The library is an excellent place to find up-to-date career information. Visit your school or public library, and research the following materials.

First, select a career CD or DVD to preview and answer these questions:

1. What is the title of your selection?

_____

2. What specific job does it describe?

_____

3. List two important facts that you learned from this material.

_____

_____

Using the *Encyclopedia of Associations,* list two trade and professional publications that you discovered in your library research.

1. Title: _____

Publisher: _____

2. Title: _____

Publisher: _____

If you are not familiar with the computerized career information system in your school or public library, ask your guidance counselor, school librarian, or public librarian to help you access it. What career information were you able to find on the computer?

_____

_____

_____

_____

Using the *Reader's Guide to Periodical Literature,* list two periodicals or magazines that contain career articles.

1. Magazine Title: _____

Article Title: _____

2. Magazine Title: _____

Article Title: _____

Name_____ **Class**_____ **Date**_____

Career Research Report

Use the following outline to write a career research report using the resources described in Chapter 5 of your textbook. Consult several sources of information for your report.

Title of occupation: _____

I. Nature of the work

   A. What work tasks are performed? _____

      _____

   B. What equipment or tools are used? _____

      _____

   C. What are the fields of specialization?_____

      _____

   D. What skills are needed? _____

      _____

   E. Working conditions/surroundings

      1. What are the physical conditions of the work site (noise levels, health hazards, stress level, cleanliness, indoors/outdoors)?

         _____

         _____

      2. What are the daily and weekly work schedules?

         _____

         _____

II. Projected earnings

   A. What are the beginning, average, and highest earnings a worker can expect?

      _____

   B. What are the benefits in addition to earnings (commissions, tips, overtime bonuses, vacations, medical care, retirement plans)?

      _____

      _____

III. Where workers are employed

   A. In which career cluster or industry is this occupation usually found?

      _____

   B. In what type of establishment and location is the work performed?

      _____

IV. Employment outlook

    A. How many workers are employed in this occupation? _____

    B. What is the projected number of openings for this occupation in the future? _____

V. Education and training

    A. What are the education and training requirements? _____

    B. What licensing or certification is required? _____

VI. Career paths

_____

_____

VII. Qualities and rewards that affect success and satisfaction

    A. What personal qualities are related to success (interests, values, goals) in this occupation?

_____

_____

    B. What accomplishments or aptitudes demonstrate ability to be successful?

_____

_____

    C. What personal rewards and satisfaction will this occupation provide or not provide?

_____

_____

VIII. Related occupations

_____

_____

_____

IX. Sources of additional information

_____

_____

_____

Evaluating Your Occupational Research

Evaluate the information you collected in the "Career Research Report" and decide whether the occupation you researched is a good choice for you by checking Yes or No after each of the following questions:

1. Number of workers employed in this occupation: _____

   Would this provide you with numerous job openings?   Yes____   No____

2. Education and training required: _____

   Does this match with your personal educational goals?   Yes____   No____

3. Outlook for this occupation: _____

   Would you have good employment in the future?   Yes____   No____

4. Earnings for this occupation: _____

   Would the earnings satisfy your lifestyle needs and wants?   Yes____   No____

5. Nature of the work: _____

   Would the job tasks satisfy your interests and values?   Yes____   No____

6. Working conditions for this job: _____

   Would these working conditions satisfy you?   Yes____   No____

7. Occupations related to this job: _____

   Would any of these occupations interest you?   Yes____   No____

   Total your numbers of Yes responses:_____

Scoring

0–3 Yes answers: You probably wouldn't care for this job area. Use the same activity questions to explore additional occupations.

4 Yes answers: You should continue to research this job. With additional research you may increase your interest in this job, or you may discover that it isn't for you.

5–7 Yes answers: You probably would enjoy this career area. You would benefit from speaking to workers in this occupation about their work and researching related occupations. Perhaps you can visit a worker in this career area at his or her place of employment.

Conducting an Informational Interview

Schedule an informational interview with someone who works in the career you are considering. Reread "The Informational Interview" section in Chapter 5 to prepare. Then use the following worksheet to record what you learn from the interview.

1. What did you find out about the nature of the work?

Skills needed to perform daily work tasks:_____

_____

Tasks related working with information, people, and tools, machines, or instruments:

_____

_____

Portion of hours spent on each of these tasks: _____

_____

Areas of specialization in this career: _____

_____

Necessary personal characteristics: _____

_____

2. What did you find out about the work environment?

Coworker characteristics: _____

_____

Manager characteristics: _____

_____

Superviser characteristics: _____

_____

Geographic locations for employers: _____

_____

Typical physical plant: _____

_____

3. What did you find out about employment opportunities?

Other employers for this career: _____

_____

Demand for qualified workers:_____

4. What did you find out about the training need for this career?

Entry-level qualifications: _____

_____

Additional training needed for advancement:_____

5. What is the future outlook for this career?

Affects of technology and changes in world economics: _____

_____

Organizations in this career area that are best positioned for future growth:

_____

6. What did you find out about the financial rewards of this career?

Beginning earnings: _____

Future earnings and advancement opportunities: _____

7. What potential career paths did you uncover in this career area? _____

_____

8. What personal perspectives did the person you interview share?

Reason for choosing this line of work: _____

_____

Best part of this job: _____

_____

Secret to success: _____

_____

Highlights of work:_____

_____

Unsatisfactory or unpleasant aspects of work: _____

_____

Advantages and disadvantages compared to similar jobs: _____

_____

Advice for new entry-level workers: _____

_____

_____

Effect of occupation on personal life: _____

_____

Best advice: _____

_____

_____

The Real Thing

You may not earn a lot of money and the working hours may not be perfect in a part-time or summer job, but this kind of job is a great way and time to learn about careers and how businesses operate. Remember, legal restrictions that are part of the Fair Labor Standards Act will limit your possibilities for employment.

Which of the following part-time or summer jobs are available in your community? Check all that apply.

Entertainment and recreation

____ recreation aide
____ arts and crafts counselor
____ entertainment at a theme park
____ art work in advertising department or window trimming
____ camp counselor
____ nature guide
____ modeling
____ sightseeing guide
____ music counselor
____ stage hand
____ ticket taker
____ golf course attendant
____ cabana attendant
____ lifeguard

Clerical

____ word processing
____ bookkeeping clerk
____ receptionist
____ typing
____ stock clerk
____ filing
____ message or mail clerk
____ cashier
____ price marking and tagging on goods

Sales

____ telephone sales
____ sporting events vendor
____ door-to-door sales
____ ice-cream vendor
____ store or demonstration sales

Service

____ baby-sitting and child care
____ packer or bagger in grocery
____ cook
____ waiter/waitress
____ dishwasher
____ errand and delivery
____ locker room attendant
____ hostess
____ chambermaid or janitor
____ car/boat/trailer cleaning

Agriculture

____ greenskeeper
____ fish hatchery worker
____ landscape laborer
____ forester aide
____ deckhand
____ lawn-service worker

Construction trades

____ laborer

1. Which of the jobs that you checked most closely match your personal orientation? (Refer to your answers in the "Identifying Your Personal Orientation" and "Connecting to Career Clusters" worksheets in Chapter 4.)

_____

_____

2. How could working at a part-time or summer job that closely matches your personal orientation help you make a long-term career decision?

_____

_____

Finding the Right Words

Chapter 5 of your textbook contains numerous terms that employers and workers use. Recognizing and understanding these terms will help you make the important career decisions you will soon face. Unscramble the terms in column B and match them to the definitions in column A.

Column A	Column B
Example: __a__ divisions into groups	a. _____ classification systems _____ flitosiacicans mystess
1. ___ to combine	**b.** _____ upaccontiola oooklut khanbdoo
2. ___ sixteen groups of careers developed by the U.S. Department of Education	**c.** _____ nnfoiet
3. ___ a cooperative program linking high school technical education college	**d.** _____ edgui orf accupontiloa oraiontplxo
4. ___ a reference book that focuses on 16 specific interest areas	**e.** _____ chet-erpp magorrp
5. ___ a record of earned academic credits	**f.** _____ nriamaofotiln eniirtwev
6. ___ a reference book published every two years by the U.S. Department of Labor that describes in detail about 250 occupations	**g.** _____ aatsddnr apaccontiolu noitacifisalc
7. ___ an organization framework for the *OOH* that contains 11 categories	**h.** _____ reacer rustlec
8. ___ a U.S. Department of Labor Internet site containing information that will assist in your employment search and increase your overall understanding of the job market	**i.** _____ gatertein
9. ___ future employment trends	**j.** _____ snittrapirc
10. ___ a meeting to discuss a career with someone in that field	**k.** _____ oymenpteml oooktlu

Checking Your Location

For each of the following statements, write **F** if the statement is more false than true. Write **T** if the statement is more true than false.

_____ **1.** The *OOH* provides detailed descriptions of more than 85 percent of all jobs in the United States.

_____ **2.** The North American Industrial System standardizes the classification systems of Canada, the United States, Mexico, and Cuba.

_____ **3.** The *GOE* focuses on 16 clearly defined interest areas.

_____ **4.** Computerized career information systems usually contain nationwide as well as state-specific career information.

_____ **5.** Classified newspaper advertisements are a poor source of local employment opportunities.

_____ **6.** By the year 2012, the U.S. will have a civilian labor force of 162.3 million workers.

_____ **7.** You can learn a lot about careers from speakers and field experience.

_____ **8.** Career exploring, career shadowing, and field experiences are good ways to observe workers in specific occupations.

_____ **9.** Co-op and internship programs are a poor way for students to determine their suitability for an occupation.

_____ **10.** Tech-prep programs offer students a foundation in many job skills and courses that are necessary for a technical education beyond high school.

_____ **11.** Learning how to use occupational information and exploring career choices now will help you make new career decisions in the future.

On a separate sheet of paper, rewrite the statements you marked false and make them true. Include the number of each statement you rewrite.

Looking Ahead: Education and Training

Chapter **6**

What Must the Worker Know?

Some occupations require similar levels of skill but have very different work tasks. For example, the mathematics skill level required for an engineering technician is the same as that for a dietitian. The language skill level required for an auto mechanic is the same as that for an ultrasound technologist.

The U.S. Department of Labor has developed six General Education Development Scales (GEDS) for measuring the mathematical and language skill requirements of occupations. Level 6 is the highest on the scale; level 1 is the lowest. Levels 1 to 3 span the skills taught in the primary grades through tenth grade. Level 4 is taught in high school and advanced middle school courses. Level 5 is taught in advanced high school courses and college. Level 6 is taught in postgraduate college courses.

Read the list of occupations that follows. Estimate the levels of math and language skills you believe are necessary for success in each occupation using the GEDS levels (1 for the lowest and 6 for the highest). Write your estimates in the spaces provided. (Your teacher has the answers.)

Occupation	Mathematics Level	Language Level
Dishwasher, kitchen helper		
Bulldozer operator		
Farm manager		
Landscape architect		
Range manager		
Auto body repairer		
Brickmason		
Computer operator		
Dental lab technician		
Diesel mechanic		
Electrician		
Mechanical engineer		
Numerical-control machine operator		
Optician		
Radiologic (X-ray) technician		
Science technician		
Telephone installer		
Ultrasound technologist		

(continued)

(continued)

Occupation	Mathematics Level	Language Level
Chemist		
Computer programmer		
Dentist		
Dietician		
Mathematician		
Numerical tool programmer		
Operations research analyst		
Physical therapist		
Physician		
Chef		
Writer or editor		
Cosmetologist		
Elementary school teacher		
Airline flight attendant		
Registered nurse		
Social worker		
Accountant		
Bank teller		
Paralegal		
Secretary		

1. How many skills levels did you mark correctly? _____

2. What occupations require a higher level of math skills than you expected?

_____

_____

3. What occupations require a higher level of language than you expected?

_____

_____

4. What occupations require a lower level of math skills than you expected?

_____

_____

5. What occupations require a lower level of language skills than you expected?

_____

_____

The Best Time to Learn Is Now!

The grades you earn today will affect your future acceptance or rejection by postsecondary schools and employers. Employers and postsecondary school admissions staff will view your high school grades as an indicator of your commitment to hard work, your ability to learn certain skills, and your interest in specific subjects. They will consider your high school achievement an important predictor of what you will do in the future.

Evaluate your academic achievement by completing the following chart. Place a check mark under the grades you earned in each subject during the last grade period. If these grades are a real evaluation of your ability in these subjects, check the Yes column. If they aren't, check the No column. If you are unsure, check the Unsure column.

School Subject	A	B	C	D	F	Yes	No	Unsure
English								
Science								
Math								
Social studies								
Foreign language								
Music								
Art								
Vocational education								
Physical education								
Other:								
Other:								

1. If you were an employer, what opinion would you have about *you* after reviewing your high school grades or transcript?

   _____

   _____

   _____

2. How can you improve an employer's opinion of you?

   _____

   _____

   _____

Education and Training After High School

This activity helps you learn about the opportunities each educational and training program described in Chapter 6 offers. Use your textbook and library resources to complete the information.

Research an apprenticeship program for an occupation that interests you and complete the following information:

Program name: _____

Program completion requirements: _____

Admissions requirements: _____

Nearest program location: _____

Program advantages: _____

Program disadvantages: _____

How the program fits my personal values, interests, aptitudes, and goals:

_____

Required high school preparation:_____

Program cost: _____

Available financial resources to pay for this program: _____

Research a vocational training program for an occupation that interests you and complete the following information:

Program name: _____

Program completion requirements: _____

Admissions requirements: _____

Nearest program location: _____

Program advantages: _____

Program disadvantages: _____

How the program fits my personal values, interests, aptitudes, and goals:

_____

Required high school preparation:_____

Program cost: _____

Available financial resources to pay for this program: _____

Research a tech-prep program for an occupation that interests you and complete the following information:

Program name: _____

Program completion requirements: _____

Admissions requirements: _____

Nearest program location: _____

Program advantages: _____

Program disadvantages: _____

How the program fits my personal values, interests, aptitudes, and goals:

_____

Required high school preparation:_____

Program cost: _____

Available financial resources to pay for this program: _____

Research an on-the-job training program for an occupation that interests you and complete the following information:

Program name: _____

Program completion requirements: _____

Admissions requirements: _____

Nearest program location: _____

Program advantages: _____

Program disadvantages: _____

How the program fits my personal values, interests, aptitudes, and goals:

_____

Required high school preparation:_____

Program cost: _____

Available financial resources to pay for this program: _____

Research a military training program for an occupation that interests you and complete the following information:

Program name: _____

Program completion requirements: _____

Admissions requirements: _____

Nearest program location: _____

Program advantages: _____

Program disadvantages: _____

How the program fits my personal values, interests, aptitudes, and goals:

_____

Required high school preparation:_____

Program cost: _____

Available financial resources to pay for this program: _____

Research a community, junior, or technical college program for an occupation that interests you and complete the following information:

Program name: _____

Program completion requirements: _____

Admissions requirements: _____

Nearest program location: _____

Program advantages: _____

Program disadvantages: _____

How the program fits my personal values, interests, aptitudes, and goals:

_____

Required high school preparation:_____

Program cost: _____

Available financial resources to pay for this program: _____

Research a four-year college or university program for an occupation that interests you and complete the following information:

Program name: _____

Program completion requirements: _____

Admissions requirements: _____

Nearest program location: _____

Program advantages: _____

Program disadvantages: _____

How the program fits my personal values, interests, aptitudes, and goals:

_____

Required high school preparation:_____

Program cost: _____

Available financial resources to pay for this program: _____

Research a graduate or professional program for an occupation that interests you and complete the following information:

Program name: _____

Program completion requirements: _____

Admissions requirements: _____

Nearest program location: _____

Program advantages: _____

Program disadvantages: _____

How the program fits my personal values, interests, aptitudes, and goals:

_____

Required high school preparation:_____

Program cost: _____

Available financial resources to pay for this program: _____

Rank the programs in the order that best fits your personal interests, aptitudes, values, occupational goals, and financial resources.

_____ Apprenticeship

_____ On-the-job training

_____ Community, junior, or technical college

_____ Vocational training

_____ Military training

_____ Four-year college or university

_____ Tech-prep

_____ Graduate or professional school

Which program would be most satisfying to you? Why?

_____

_____

_____

_____

_____

Using a College Directory

Visit your high school library, and use one of the directories mentioned in Chapter 6 of your textbook to complete the following activity. Select three postsecondary schools or programs that you would be interested in attending. Compare them according to the following factors, and rate each school according to how well it meets your requirements. Let 1 be the highest rating and 3 be the lowest rating.

Postsecondary School Comparison

Factor	Your Requirements	Ratings		
		School 1 Name:	School 2 Name:	School Name:
Tuition/fees for one year				
Room and board fees				
SAT verbal and math scores				
ACT scores				
Application deadline				
Number of freshmen applicants				
Number freshmen accepted				
Students/faculty ratio				
Level of competitiveness				
Programs of study offered				
Financial aid available				
Location of school				
Total enrollment				
Average class size				
Accreditation				
Public/private school				

Which school would you select on the basis of your requirements?

_____

Why?

_____

Based on your school achievement, which school would accept you?

_____

Why?

_____

Finding the Right Words

Chapter 6 of your textbook contains numerous terms that employers and workers use. Recognizing and understanding these terms will help you make the important career decisions you will soon face.

Unscramble the vocabulary terms, and complete the following sentences.

1. LIANICFAN DAI Pell Grants, Perkins Loans, and college work-study programs are examples of the available _____ to pay for school.

2. TEMIDOHCLA Using a _____ approach is best when you are trying to figure out what training you will need to achieve your career goals.

3. PTADA In order to _____ to a changing workplace, workers will require education throughout their lives.

4. PLOYEMNTME TURSCURET The type of jobs within an organization is known as its _____.

5. PPATICESHIPREN An _____ is a relationship between an employer and a worker during which the worker learns a trade.

6. ILDUGS _____ are unions of craft workers.

7. ENOP-SADMNOISIS COPILY Most public two-year colleges have an _____.

8. JNEYOUR ERWORK A _____ is a certified, experienced, skilled craft worker who has successfully completed his or her apprenticeship.

9. OPRIREARYT HSCOOL A _____ is a school that is privately owned and operated for profit.

10. TECHLCANI OOHSCL A _____ is a two-year institution that offers occupational programs intended to prepare students for immediate employment in fields related to engineering and the physical sciences.

11. FCCDDEETIA An _____ college or educational program has met certain minimum standards for its facilities and program of study.

12. RRESDENCECOPON COUSESR _____ are also known as home study courses.

13. OBJ PCORS The _____ is a federally administered, national employment and training program serving severely disadvantaged youth 16 to 21 years of age.

14. DETNTUS-YACFLUT AOTIR An important number to look at when you are evaluating postsecondary schools is the _____.

15. NO HET OBJ INGTRAIN _____ comprises a wide range of education and training provided by employers for their employees.

16. LAURBACCEATEA EREEGD _____ is sometimes called a bachelor's degree or an undergraduate degree.

17. VERUNTYSII A _____, the largest type of institution of higher learning, is composed of several undergraduate colleges and graduate schools for advanced study.

Name_____ Class_____ Date_____

Checking Your Location

For each of the following statements, write **F** if the statement is more false than true. Write **T** if the statement is more true than false.

_____ **1.** Job opportunities for highly trained and educated workers are increasing, as are those for unskilled workers.

_____ **2.** Some form of postsecondary education and training will be required for 75 percent of all job classifications during and beyond the 2000s.

_____ **3.** The risk of unemployment is higher for high school dropouts than for high school graduates.

_____ **4.** Employers rarely contact a job seeker's high school to obtain information about grades and attendance.

_____ **5.** An increasing number of employers are testing job seekers to determine their proficiency in basic high school skills.

_____ **6.** Although English usage and reading comprehension are needed at some level in all occupations, mathematics is not.

_____ **7.** Today's apprenticeship programs usually require about four years of training but may range from one to six years.

_____ **8.** Tech-prep students are expected to graduate from high school prepared for both further training and work.

_____ **9.** More than 90 percent of today's high school graduates enter some form of educational program after high school.

_____ **10.** It is important to be very selective in choosing a postsecondary school because of the wide range of quality and the high cost of tuition.

_____ **11.** The Job Corps is a federally administered employment and training program that serves severely disadvantaged young people aged 16 to 21.

_____ **12.** A major share of postsecondary education is provided by public and private colleges that award associate degrees after two years of full-time study.

_____ **13.** There are more than 3,300 accredited colleges, community colleges, and universities in the United States.

_____ **14.** State universities are supported by public funding and are usually more expensive than private universities.

_____ **15.** To obtain a graduate degree, a student must meet the requirements established by the college or school awarding the degree.

On a separate sheet of paper, rewrite the statements you marked false and make them true. Include the number of each statement you rewrite.

Expressing Yourself: Effective Communication Chapter 7

Encode, Decode

On the following chart, keep track of whom you communicate with, how you communicate, and how much time you spend encoding (changing thoughts, feelings, and ideas into words) and decoding (interpreting symbols as the sender intended) messages from the time you get up in the morning until you go to bed that night. Include television, telephone, and computer use. A sample entry is provided.

Location and Time of Day	What did you read?	What did you write?	To whom did you listen?	To whom did you speak?
7:00 a.m., home				Mom, 15 min.

How much time did you spend reading?_____ Writing?_____

Listening?_____ Speaking?_____

Which did you do the most?_____ The least?_____

Which of the four was the easiest to understand? _____

Which was most difficult? _____

Name _____ **Class** _____ **Date** _____

Body Language—What Does It Mean?

Effective oral communication skill requires an understanding of the importance of body language when communicating. Body language depends on the situation and must be interpreted in context with the situation.

Many nonverbal gestures have almost universal meanings. What do the following gestures mean to you? Write your answer in the blank provided.

Waving your hand: _____

Holding your nose: _____

Clapping your hands: _____

Crossing your fingers: _____

Holding your thumbs up: _____

Blowing a kiss: _____

Nodding your head up and down: _____

Shrugging your shoulders: _____

Tapping your fingers: _____

Clenching your fist: _____

Holding your thumb down: _____

Shaking your head sideways: _____

Hugging: _____

Body language must be interpreted as it relates to different situations. Observe someone using body language and answer the following questions:

1. What is the situation?

   _____

2. What is this person doing with his or her arms and hands?

   _____

3. What is this person doing with his or her legs and feet?

   _____

4. What is this person doing with his or her eyes?

   _____

5. How is this person postured?

   _____

Name_____ Class_____ Date_____

Are You a Good Listener?

When you have a full-time job, it will be important to listen to your boss and your coworkers. If you are a poor listener, you risk responding incorrectly, and you might come away with a very different message from the one intended. Poor listening can lead to misunderstandings, mistakes, and bad working relationships.

Evaluate yourself as a listener by answering the following questions. There are no correct or incorrect answers. Your responses will help you understand yourself as a listener.

How would you describe yourself as a listener?

___ Superior   ___ Below average

___ Excellent   ___ Poor

___ Above average   ___ Terrible

___ Average

How would the following people rate you as a listener on a scale of 0 (low) to 100 (high)?

___ Someone who tells you what to do   ___ Your spouse or mother

___ Your best friend   ___ Your brother or sister

___ A classmate

How often do you engage in the following bad listening habits? Put a check mark in the column that best describes how often you engage in each bad habit.

Listening Habit	Almost Always	Usually	Sometimes	Seldom	Almost Never
Calling a subject uninteresting					
Criticizing a speaker's delivery or mannerisms					
Becoming overly enthusiastic about something a speaker says					
Listening primarily for facts					
Trying to outline everything					
Faking attention to the speaker					
Allowing distractions to interfere with communication					
Avoiding difficult material					
Letting emotion-laden words make you angry					
Wasting the advantage of thinking by daydreaming					
Column total:					

For every "Almost Always" checked, give yourself a score of 2. (2 X __ = __)

For every "Usually" checked, give yourself a score of 4. (4 X __ = __)

For every "Sometimes" checked, give yourself a score of 6. (6 X __ = __)

For every "Seldom" checked, give yourself a score of 8. (8 X __ = __)

For every "Almost Never" checked, give yourself a score of 10. (10 X __ = __)

Enter your total score here: _____

How did you rate as a listener? (Use the following scoring scale.)

Scoring: Less than 21 = terrible; 22–41 = poor; 42–55 = below average; 56–71 = average; 72–85 = above average; 86–93 = excellent; 94–100 = superior.

Based on the results of this quiz, which areas need the most improvement?

_____

_____

What is one listening habit you would like to improve?

_____

Keep a log to track your efforts in improving your listening skills.

Responding

In your textbook, you learned that *paraphrasing* helps people communicate with one another. Paraphrasing is repeating the speaker's ideas or thoughts in your own words. It is a verbal reflection of what you heard the speaker say. You make no suggestions, give no advice, and ask no questions. You encourage the speaker to tell you more. It is useful when you want to help someone talk their way through the solution of a problem.

Ask two classmates or close friends to participate in this activity. Ask one person to be the observer and the other to be the speaker.

Speaker's name: _____

Observer's name: _____

The speaker will talk to you for five minutes about what he or she hopes will happen in the next five years. You will be the listener who responds to the speaker. Keep these points in mind:

- Listen to the speaker with an open mind.

- Make a conscious effort to keep your own thoughts from interfering with attending to the speaker (we think much faster than we can talk.)

- Concentrate on what the speaker is saying and pay attention to the speaker's nonverbal cues.

- Watch your own body language. Keep your hands and feet still.

- Look the speaker in the eye, but do not stare.

- Encourage the speaker to keep talking. (Paraphrase, ask the speaker "Will you tell me more about that?" or say "I don't understand. Please clarify that for me.")

The observer gives you feedback on your use of communication helpers and stoppers using the Observer's Record Sheet.

Observer's Record Sheet

Did the listener	Yes	No	Sometimes
Paraphase?			
Encourage?			
Probe question?			
Stay receptive?			
Interrupt the speaker?			
Judge the speaker?			
Communicate the message as received?			
Leave out part of the message?			
Add to the message?			
Seem attentive with good eye contact?			
Seem attentive with good body posture?			

At the end of the session, ask the speaker the following questions:

1. What, if anything, did I do that made you feel as if I were listening to you?

_____

_____

2. How did you feel as I paraphrased what you were saying?

_____

_____

Ask the observer to share his or her observations of you in your role as listener. Then respond to these questions:

1. How did you feel as you tried to paraphrase the speaker?

_____

_____

2. Did you have the urge to say your own thoughts?

_____

_____

3. Was it difficult to tune in to what the speaker was saying?

_____

_____

4. Did you draw conclusions before listening to the speaker's entire message?

_____

_____

5. What did you learn about listening and responding in this activity?

_____

_____

Conflict Resolution

In the workplace (as in any situation with personal interaction) there is a potential for conflict. Different priorities, biases, expertise, and interests can result in disagreements and opposition to issues. When anger or irritation is expressed, the conflict must be resolved.

The successful negotiation of conflict focuses on problems, not feelings or personalities. It relies on effective interpersonal skills and a clear understanding of the approach demanded by the circumstances. All beliefs, opinions, or viewpoints are in the open.

Assume the role of negotiator in the following situation:

> Rita and Betty live in the same neighborhood, own automobiles, and drive 15 miles each way to work the evening shift at CDS Enterprises. Last month, Rita and Betty decided that they could save considerable money by forming a car pool. Now they take turns driving to work.
>
> When Rita drives, they arrive at CDS only five minutes before starting time, which caused them to be seven minutes late last Friday when traffic was heavy. The supervisor gave them a warning. When Betty drives, they arrive at CDS about 40 minutes before starting time. Betty enjoys drinking coffee with her coworkers in the employee lounge before her shift begins. Rita would rather drink coffee at home with her husband. The two women had an argument about this situation on the way to work this evening and didn't speak to each other on the way home.

1. What is Rita's view of the conflict? (How does she feel and what does she want?)

_____

_____

2. What is Betty's view of the conflict? (How does she feel and what does she want?)

_____

_____

3. Why would agreement benefit both parties?

_____

_____

4. Identify a belief, opinion, or viewpoint on which both parties agree.

_____

_____

5. Identify beliefs, opinions, or viewpoints on which both parties disagree.

_____

_____

6. Offer a win-win solution or a compromise to the conflict.

_____

_____

7. How would your resolution of the conflict work in a real-life situation?

_____

_____

Think of a disagreement you have had with a friend or family member.

1. What did you do to resolve the disagreement?

_____

_____

_____

_____

2. How did you feel about the disagreement and the resolution?

_____

_____

_____

_____

Listen to a nightly news broadcast or scan the local newspapers for stories about conflict. Choose one conflict and describe what could be done to resolve it.

_____

_____

_____

_____

_____

_____

_____

Key to Success: When you have a disagreement with someone, focus on points of agreement before discussing your differences.

Finding the Right Words

Write a paragraph about communication in the workplace using 12 of the vocabulary words from Chapter 7. Circle the words you use in the following list.

active vocabulary	context	monitor
arbitrator	empathy	negotiation
bandwidth	facilitate	nonverbal communication
business letter	FAX machines	paraphrasing
communication	inflection	recognition vocabulary
compromise	memorandums	videoconferencing
		World Wide Web

_____

_____

_____

_____

_____

_____

_____

_____

_____

_____

_____

_____

_____

_____

_____

_____

_____

_____

_____

_____

_____

_____

Checking Your Location

For each of the following statements, write **F** if the statement is more false than true. Write **T** if the statement is more true than false.

___ **1.** Communication is an integral part of every industry and business in the United States.

___ **2.** Job knowledge ranks slightly below communication skills as a factor in career success.

___ **3.** The average worker spends most of his or her time speaking.

___ **4.** Chinese is the most commonly used language in the international world of work.

___ **5.** Your recognition vocabulary will include at least 80,000 words by the time you leave high school.

___ **6.** It is usually safer to begin using new words in your writing rather than in conversation.

___ **7.** Effective communication exists when the receiver interprets the sender's message as the sender intended.

___ **8.** Speaking is the most-often-used method of communicating policies, procedures, and concepts in the workplace.

___ **9.** The average employee spends one-and-a-half to two hours each workday doing some form of reading.

___ **10.** Skimming material will never provide all that you need to completely understand printed materials.

___ **11.** Successful interpersonal relationships are built on mutual trust, acceptance, empathy, and understanding.

___ **12.** Effective communication is important in all interpersonal aspects of life.

___ **13.** All groups have some form of organization, rules for establishing leadership, and expectations regarding member behavior.

___ **14.** Leaders of democratic groups rarely rely on members of the group during the decision-making process.

___ **15.** Each person involved in a conflict has personal biases, priorities, expertise, and interests that affect the points of agreement and create outright opposition on many issues.

On a separate sheet of paper, rewrite the statements you marked false and make them true. Include the number of each statement you rewrite.

Conducting the Job Search

Chapter **8**

Learning How to Conduct a Successful Job Search

Ask a parent or friend who is employed the following questions:

1. What method did you use to get your present job? (Mark all that apply.)

   ___ Applied directly to the employer

   ___ Contacted professional or trade
   organizations

   ___ Responded to help-wanted ads

   ___ Used a private employment agency

   ___ Networked

   ___ Used school placement services

   ___ Used the State Bureau of Employment
   Services

2. If you needed to look for employment again, which methods would you use? Why?

   _____

   _____

   _____

   _____

3. What did you do that made your job search successful?

   _____

   _____

   _____

   _____

4. What was the most difficult part about getting your present job?

   _____

   _____

   _____

   _____

5. Why do you believe you were selected over other applicants for your present job?

   _____

   _____

   _____

   _____

Now it's your turn to answer some questions. What is one job you want to have when you graduate from high school?

_____

List all the requirements for the job you named:

_____

_____

_____

_____

_____

Think about the courses in which you receive the best grades, the courses you took that are job-related, school activities you like, tasks you have done well in the past, and good things people have said about you or your work. Now list the benefits you would offer an employer who hires you for the job you named.

_____

_____

_____

_____

_____

_____

Identify three employers in your area who would hire someone for this job:

_____

_____

_____

Telephoning the Employer

Most successful job searches require careful planning. Review the case of Raymond Wilson.

Raymond is a senior at Martin Luther King High School. He wants to obtain part-time employment at a trucking company and eventually become a long-distance truck driver. Using the yellow pages of the telephone book, Raymond turns to the T section. He discovers 60 major headings from "Truck — Air-conditioning Equipment" to "Trucks — Motor." He turns to the heading "Truck — Motor Freight" and finds six trucking companies listed. Raymond decides to phone the J&R Transit Company. Listen to his conversation:

> *Raymond:* Hello. I'm looking for a part-time job, and I want to work for your company. Do you have any openings today?
>
> *Receptionist:* I'm very sorry, but the person in charge of hiring is out of the office today.
>
> *Raymond:* Thank you very much. I'll call back next week.

Raymond knows the career path he wants to follow and he has used the job-search method of applying directly to the employer. He was very polite on the telephone, but he does not know any more about who is responsible for hiring or what procedures the J&R Transit Company uses to hire employees than he did before he made the telephone call.

1. What information should Raymond have sought from the receptionist? (Review "Applying Directly to the Employer" in your textbook.)

   _____

2. What could Raymond have said to improve his telephone introduction?

   _____

3. What are some questions he might have asked the receptionist?

   _____

4. What personal information should Raymond have on paper when he calls back? Why?

   _____

Write a telephone introduction that you would use to introduce yourself to one of the employers you identified in the last question of the preceding worksheet, "Learning How to Conduct a Successful Job Search."

_____

_____

_____

_____

Help-Wanted Advertisements

Almost 46 percent of job seekers use the advertisements in their local newspaper to find job leads. Although few workers are hired through advertisements, ads provide helpful information for the job search. The following table lists some of the most common abbreviations found in job advertisements.

Abbreviations	Meaning
Eve	Evening, night
EOE	Equal Opportunity Employment
F/T	Full-time
Hr	Hour
M/F	Monday through Friday
P/T	Part-time
Ref Req	References required
Lic	License
Xllent	Excellent

Select one job you want to have from the classified advertisements in the Sunday edition of your local newspaper. Then answer the following questions:

1. Under what category of work does the ad appear? _____

2. Who is the employer?_____

3. What is the company's product or service?_____

4. What position or positions are open? _____

5. What do the abbreviations in the ad stand for? (Refer to the previous table for help.)

   _____

   _____

6. What qualifications do you have for the position?

   _____

7. If you do not have relevant work experience for the job, what have you done that could substitute for that experience?

   _____

8. What additional information would you need before deciding whether you qualify for this job?

   _____

9. What responsibilities would you have on this job?

   _____

10. How do you apply for the job? _____

11. Whom do you contact to apply for the position? _____

Using One-Stop Career Centers

The U.S. Employment Service provides free employment assistance. Visit your local office and ask to interview an employment counselor.

1. What is the name of the employment counselor? ＿＿＿＿＿＿＿＿＿＿＿＿＿＿＿＿＿＿＿＿＿

2. How do the counselors decide which employment candidates will be sent to interview for specific jobs?

＿＿＿＿＿＿＿＿＿＿＿＿＿＿＿＿＿＿＿＿＿＿＿＿＿＿＿＿＿＿＿＿＿＿＿＿＿＿

＿＿＿＿＿＿＿＿＿＿＿＿＿＿＿＿＿＿＿＿＿＿＿＿＿＿＿＿＿＿＿＿＿＿＿＿＿＿

3. What type of testing is available for job seekers at this agency?

＿＿＿＿＿＿＿＿＿＿＿＿＿＿＿＿＿＿＿＿＿＿＿＿＿＿＿＿＿＿＿＿＿＿＿＿＿＿

＿＿＿＿＿＿＿＿＿＿＿＿＿＿＿＿＿＿＿＿＿＿＿＿＿＿＿＿＿＿＿＿＿＿＿＿＿＿

4. What special assistance does the agency offer to veterans?

＿＿＿＿＿＿＿＿＿＿＿＿＿＿＿＿＿＿＿＿＿＿＿＿＿＿＿＿＿＿＿＿＿＿＿＿＿＿

＿＿＿＿＿＿＿＿＿＿＿＿＿＿＿＿＿＿＿＿＿＿＿＿＿＿＿＿＿＿＿＿＿＿＿＿＿＿

5. What special assistance does the agency offer to the physically challenged?

＿＿＿＿＿＿＿＿＿＿＿＿＿＿＿＿＿＿＿＿＿＿＿＿＿＿＿＿＿＿＿＿＿＿＿＿＿＿

＿＿＿＿＿＿＿＿＿＿＿＿＿＿＿＿＿＿＿＿＿＿＿＿＿＿＿＿＿＿＿＿＿＿＿＿＿＿

6. What services does the agency offer to ex-offenders who are seeking to make the transition from prison to civilian life?

＿＿＿＿＿＿＿＿＿＿＿＿＿＿＿＿＿＿＿＿＿＿＿＿＿＿＿＿＿＿＿＿＿＿＿＿＿＿

＿＿＿＿＿＿＿＿＿＿＿＿＿＿＿＿＿＿＿＿＿＿＿＿＿＿＿＿＿＿＿＿＿＿＿＿＿＿

7. What federally funded programs does the agency administer?

＿＿＿＿＿＿＿＿＿＿＿＿＿＿＿＿＿＿＿＿＿＿＿＿＿＿＿＿＿＿＿＿＿＿＿＿＿＿

＿＿＿＿＿＿＿＿＿＿＿＿＿＿＿＿＿＿＿＿＿＿＿＿＿＿＿＿＿＿＿＿＿＿＿＿＿＿

Ask the employment counselor for an employment application. Fill it out and return it to the counselor.

1. For what type of job did you qualify? ＿＿＿＿＿＿＿＿＿＿＿＿＿＿＿＿＿＿＿＿＿＿＿

2. To what job classification did the employment counselor assign you? ＿＿＿＿＿＿＿＿＿＿

3. What job openings are available in your job classification?

＿＿＿＿＿＿＿＿＿＿＿＿＿＿＿＿＿＿＿＿＿＿＿＿＿＿＿＿＿＿＿＿＿＿＿＿＿＿

＿＿＿＿＿＿＿＿＿＿＿＿＿＿＿＿＿＿＿＿＿＿＿＿＿＿＿＿＿＿＿＿＿＿＿＿＿＿

Name_____ **Class**_____ **Date**_____

Preparing Your Personal Data Sheet

Before you begin this activity, review the section called "Preparing a Personal Data Sheet" in your textbook. Then complete the following personal data sheet. Be thorough and careful as you fill in the information. Remember that a personal data sheet lists accurate information about you that is important to employers. You will be asked for this information when you fill out a job application or are interviewed for a job.

Personal Data Sheet

Personal Information

Your full name:_____

Social Security number: __ __ __ - __ __ - __ __ __ __

Address: _____

Phone number: _____ Date available for employment: _____

Date of birth: Month:_____ Day:_____ Year:_____

Marital status: Single   Married

Height:_____Weight:_____lbs.

Citizenship status:_____

Name and phone number of people to contact in an emergency:

   a. Name: _____

      Address: _____

      Phone number: _____

      Relationship: _____

   b. Name: _____

      Address: _____

      Phone number: _____

      Relationship: _____

   c. Name: _____

      Address: _____

      Phone number: _____

      Relationship: _____

Educational Background

Name of high school: _____

School address:_____

_____

School phone number: _____

Present status as a student: Part-time   Full-time   Graduate

Grade point average:_____ Class rank: _____

Dates of attendance: From: _____ To:_____

Course of study: General   Vocational   College preparatory

Extracurricular activities (clubs, sports):

_____

_____

Awards or honors:

_____

_____

Favorite subjects:

_____

_____

Part-time or Full-time Work Experience

    a. Name of company: _____

        Dates employed: _____

        Position: _____

        Responsibilities: _____

        Wages or salary: Starting: _____ Final:_____

        Reason for leaving: _____

    b. Name of company: _____

        Dates employed: _____

        Position: _____

        Responsibilities: _____

        Wages or salary: Starting: _____ Final: _____

        Reason for leaving: _____

Volunteer Work

    a. Name of organization: _____

        Reason for volunteering for this organization: _____

        Duties or responsibilities:

_____

_____

    b. Name of organization: _____

        Reason for volunteering for this organization: _____

        Duties or responsibilities:

_____

_____

Future Educational Goals

Career/job goal:

_____

_____

_____

References

  a. Name: _____

     Address: _____

     Job title: _____

     Phone number: _____

     Relationship: _____

  b. Name: _____

     Address: _____

     Job title: _____

     Phone number: _____

     Relationship: _____

  c. Name: _____

     Address: _____

     Job title: _____

     Phone number: _____

     Relationship: _____

Major qualifications for the position (skills such as typing, operating equipment):

_____

_____

_____

Leisure-time activities and hobbies:

_____

_____

Finding the Right Words

Decipher the Chapter 8 vocabulary terms hidden below by using the following key. The first one has been done for you.

Key:

a	b	c	d	e	f	g	h	i	j	k	l	m	n	o	p	q	r	s	t	u	v	w	x	y	z
1	2	3	4	5	6	7	8	9	10	11	12	13	14	15	16	17	18	19	20	21	22	23	24	25	26

Example:

1. e m p l o y m e n t s e r v i c e
5 13 16 12 15 25 13 5 14 20 19 5 18 22 9 3 5

2. _ _ _ _ _ _ _ _
2 12 9 14 4 1 4 19

3. _ _ _ _ _ _
18 5 19 21 13 5

4. _ _ _ _ _ _ _ _ _ _ _ _ _ _ _ _
16 5 18 19 15 14 1 12 4 1 20 1 19 8 5 5 20

5. _ _ _ _ _ _ _ _ _ _
18 5 6 5 18 5 14 3 5 19

6. _ _ _ _ _ _ _
10 15 2 12 5 1 4

7. _ _ _ _ _ _ _ _ _
10 15 2 19 5 1 18 3 8

8. _ _ _ _ _ _ _ _ _ _
18 5 19 21 13 5 2 1 14 11

9. _ _ _ _ _ _ _ _ _ _ _
3 15 22 5 18 12 5 20 20 5 18

10. _ _ _ _ _ _ _ _
10 15 2 6 1 9 18 19

11. _ _ _ _ _ _ _ _ _
10 15 2 13 1 18 11 5 20

12. _ _ _ _ _ _ _ _ _ _ _ _ _ _ _ _ _ _
19 3 18 5 5 14 9 14 7 9 14 20 5 18 22 9 5 23

13. _ _ _ _ _ _ _ _ _ _
14 5 20 23 15 18 11 9 14 7

14. _ _ _ _ _ _ _ _ _ _ _ _ _ _ _ _ _
6 21 14 3 20 9 15 14 1 12 18 5 19 21 13 5

Checking Your Location

For each of the following statements, write **F** if the statement is more false than true. Write **T** if the statement is more true than false.

____ **1.** The least successful method for a job search is networking.

____ **2.** The Sunday edition of most major newspapers carries advertisements about job openings from organizations and employment agencies.

____ **3.** Employment agency fees are always paid by the applicant.

____ **4.** It takes an average of six to eight weeks for an employer to fill a position.

____ **5.** You write a personal data sheet for your own use; you do not give it to an employer.

____ **6.** Employers thoroughly read all resumes sent to them by potential employees.

____ **7.** Cover letters should always be written for a specific employer and position.

____ **8.** The U.S. Department of Labor estimates that a bad hiring decision costs a company one-third of the new hire's annual salary.

____ **9.** You have to pay a fee and pass an employment test to use the services at One-Stop Career Centers.

____ **10.** Job seekers are more likely to find the type of employment for which they are qualified if they learn specific job-search skills.

____ **11.** Having a personal data sheet simplifies the task of filling out job applications.

____ **12.** A functional resume emphasizes dates of employment and steady growth.

____ **13.** Using job lead cards and making a job file are effective methods for job seekers to organize their job-search information.

____ **14.** Nationwide, only 50 percent of all newly hired employees last more than six months.

On a separate sheet of paper, rewrite the statements you marked false and make them true. Include the number of each statement you rewrite.

Applying and Interviewing for a Job

Chapter **9**

What Should Shonda Do?

Shonda knows that she can be a good salesperson at the mall. She likes to talk with people, enjoys helping them, and likes the idea of a job where she can dress well. Although she is only 17, people tell her that she is very mature and that she relates well to adults.

Shonda spent the entire weekend visiting mall stores and asking to speak with the person in charge of employment. She can hardly believe that she completed 16 job applications. If being thorough, neat, and interested help people get jobs, she will have one soon.

Three days have gone by, and Shonda still hasn't heard back from any of the stores in which she applied. She feels very discouraged.

1. What can Shonda do to follow up with the applications she made?

_____

2. Do you think Shonda should wait for the employers she contacted to offer an interview or should she make additional applications? Why or why not?

_____

_____

Review the section called "Job Application Forms" in your textbook and answer the following questions about job applications.

1. A question on the job application asks for your expected pay. What should you put in the blank?

_____

_____

2. Keeping in mind that many teenagers are interviewed the same day they fill out an application, what should you do to prepare to fill out job applications?

_____

_____

3. If you were giving a friend advice about filling out a job application, what three things would you tell him or her?

_____

_____

_____

_____

Being Informed About the Company

"Mrs. Stolz will see you now, Mr. Garcia," the receptionist says. Pete Garcia feels a little nervous as he walks into the interviewing office. He can only hope that Mrs. Stolz will be as pleasant as the receptionist in the outer office.

Mrs. Stolz stands up and walks around her large mahogany desk to shake his hand. "Good morning, Mr. Garcia," she says. "I'm looking forward to our interview. Let's sit at the table by the window. It's more comfortable than sitting at the desk."

As they sit down, Mrs. Stolz asks Pete, "Why do you want to work for our company, Mr. Garcia?" Pete tells her that he read about several insurance companies and talked with employees and customers of the different companies. This company was growing, the employees liked working there, and the customers were satisfied. As he continues talking, the words come more easily.

As Pete leaves the office to go home, he feels satisfied. He knows that it was a good interview.

1. What verbal messages did Pete send to Mrs. Stolz that indicated that he was informed about the company?

   _____

   _____

2. What verbal messages did Pete send to Mrs. Stolz that he had a positive opinion about the company?

   _____

   _____

Select one employer in your community that you might like to work for when you get a full-time job. Using one or more of the sources listed in Table 9.1 on page 194 of your textbook, learn all you can about the company.

1. What is the company's product or service? _____

2. What were the annual sales last year?_____

3. How many employees does the company have? _____

4. How long has the company been in business? _____

5. Who owns the company? _____

6. What is its financial standing? _____

7. What is its reputation as an employer? _____

8. How would this information help you in an interview and in making a decision about accepting a job offer?

   _____

   _____

Appearance Makes an Impression

Most companies are concerned about the image they want to present to the public and about their employ-ees' compatibility with that image. Most employers believe that employees who have pride in themselves will have pride in the company for which they work. When you go to an interview, be well-groomed and neatly attired, and project an image of success. Consider the image that each of the following job candi-dates projects to potential employers.

Melissa, who is 17, is very nervous about her first important job interview with a large insurance company. She tries to overcome her youthful image with clothes and makeup that would be suitable for a rock star. She doesn't get the job. After Melissa learns the true purpose of the job interview, she changes to a more conservative image and is successful.

Eugene, who is also 17, didn't find work as a data processor right away. Initially he dressed for interviews as he usually dresses: with an earring and a design shaved into his very short hair. He found that most hir-ing managers are conservative and have middle-class values, and he felt that they were uncomfortable with him. He did find success when dressed in a suit and tie, with the hairstyle and image of a well-groomed working man.

1. What opinion do you think the first interviewer had of Melissa?

_____

2. What opinion do you think the first interviewer had of Eugene?

_____

3. People dress as they perceive themselves. Which of the two job seekers has the weakest self-image? What indications support your position?

_____

_____

_____

4. Consider your present image. How would your appearance (hair, clothing, posture, fingernails, shoes, teeth, accessories) measure up in an employment interview? Explain your answer.

_____

_____

_____

5. If you were a career counselor, what advice would you give Melissa?

_____

_____

_____

6. What advice would you give Eugene?

_____

_____

_____

Part-time and Summertime Jobs

Your first job will probably be a part-time or summer job. The job possibilities are more limited than they will be when you have more education and training, but employers' expectations will not change. Use the information you have learned thus far when applying for part-time or summer employment.

Prepare for the interview as if it were the most important job of your life. The success of most interviews is determined by the skill demonstrated in communicating answers to specific questions. The interviewer will already have formed an opinion of you based on your job application or resume. He or she will be looking you over and checking information about your school attendance, attitude, work values, goals, job experience, and job expectations.

Imagine that you have been invited to interview for a summer job. Write your responses to the following interview questions:

1. Why do you want this job? Why do you want to work for our organization?

_____

_____

2. What can you contribute to our company that would make us hire you over others?

_____

_____

3. We need someone with experience. What kind of experience can you offer us?

_____

_____

4. What high school courses have you taken that will help you on this job? What were your grades? What was your GPA?

_____

_____

5. What are your strongest and weakest skills for this job?

_____

6. Tell me about yourself.

_____

_____

7. How many days of school did you miss this year? What about last year?

_____

8. Do you prefer working closely with others or mostly by yourself?

_____

9. How did previous employers or teachers treat you?

_____

_____

10. What would previous employers or teachers say about you?

_____

_____

11. What will your answer to question 1 tell the employer about your goals?

_____

_____

12. What will your answers to question 7 tell the employer about your reliability?

_____

13. What will your answers to questions 9 and 10 tell the employer about your attitude?

_____

_____

14. What will your answer to question 8 tell the employer about your ability to get along with others in work relationships?

_____

_____

15. Which of the following would be easy for you in a part-time or summer job? Which would be difficult? Write your answer (**easy** or **difficult**) in the space provided.

Taking and following orders from supervisors _____

Expressing a positive attitude _____

Following instructions and handling criticism _____

Being responsible and using care in handling tools and equipment _____

Thinking before speaking _____

Listening carefully _____

Being courteous and respectful to customers at all times_____

Performing a full day's work_____

Responding to stress in an acceptable manner _____

Being reliable and on time _____

Being pleasant in appearance and personal hygiene _____

Keeping your personal life from interfering with the job_____

Cooperating with coworkers_____

Following policies and procedures _____

16. How many items in question 15 would you find easy? _____

How many would be difficult? _____

Look closely at those you marked difficult. What can you do to improve in these areas?

_____

_____

_____

17. List four skills you will bring to a part-time or summer job. (Review the Chapter 2 worksheet, "Skills—Now and for Tomorrow," for ideas.)

a. _____

b. _____

c. _____

d. _____

18. List four work values you will bring to a part-time summer job. (Review the "Examining Your Work Values" worksheet in Chapter 3 for ideas.)

a. _____

b. _____

c. _____

d. _____

19. How could working at a part-time or summer job that closely matches your personal orientation help you make a long-term decision?

_____

_____

Key to Success: Your search for summer work should be under way by spring break.

Finding the Right Words

Chapter 9 of your textbook contains numerous terms that employers and workers use. Recognizing and understanding these terms will help you make the important career decisions you will soon face. Fill in the missing vowels in the vocabulary terms in column B, and match them with the definitions in column A.

Column A	Column B
1. ___ a statement containing information that employers require before hiring new employees	**a.** F _ _ r L _ b _ r St _ nd _ rds _ ct
2. ___ laws that protect all workers, including laws governing the employment of minors	**b.** c _ v _ l s _ rv _ c _ ex _ m _ n _ t _ _ ns
3. ___ a document that states that you don't have an infectious disease	**c.** h _ _ lth c _ rt _ f _ c _ t _
4. ___ a form from the Immigration and Naturalization Service or the Department of Labor	**d.** j _ b _ ppl _ c _ t _ _ n f _ rm
5. ___ a type of insurance that pays financial losses if an employee fails to perform his or her duty or is guilty of theft	**e.** _ mpl _ ym _ nt _ l _ g _ b _ l _ ty v _ r _ f _ c _ t _ _ n f _ rm
6. ___ a serious crime	**f.** b _ nd
7. ___ government preemployment tests	**g.** f _ l _ ny
8. ___ true and supported by facts	**h.** _ n _ t _ _ t _ v _
9. ___ readiness and ability to take the first steps in any undertaking	**i.** v _ l _ d
10. ___ the workers who are responsible for recruiting and hiring new employees	**j.** f _ _ r _ mpl _ ym _ nt pr _ g r _ m
11. ___ a program that helps employers actively seek to hire minorities	**k.** j _ b _ ff _ r
12. ___ an employer's formal proposal of employment	**l.** h _ m _ n r _ s _ _ _ rc _ s d _ p _ rtm _ nt
13. ___ a document required for employees under 18 years old in most nonfarm jobs	**m.** w _ rk p _ rm _ t
14. ___ an investigation of former employers, schools, and references	**n.** b _ ckgr _ _ _ nd ch _ ck

Checking Your Location

For each of the following statements, write **F** if the statement is more false than true. Write **T** if the statement is more true than false.

____ **1.** Job applications become legal documents after they are signed and dated.

____ **2.** You no longer need a work permit when you turn 16 years old.

____ **3.** The applicant's skill in communicating answers to specific questions determines the success of most job interviews.

____ **4.** The Civil Rights Act of 1964 contains the Equal Employment Opportunity Law.

____ **5.** Some companies like to use temporary help because it saves them the expense of hiring full-time employees that they will need for only a short time.

____ **6.** Employers cannot use job applications to screen out unqualified applicants before job interviews are conducted.

____ **7.** The Fair Labor Standards Act protects most workers but does not include laws governing the employment of minors.

____ **8.** The federal government cannot limit or regulate the right of foreign citizens to be employed in the United States.

____ **9.** Most employers consider preemployment tests to be an objective and unbiased method for evaluating potential employees.

____ **10.** Learning all you can about an employer's business operations will help you make a wiser decision if you are offered a job.

____ **11.** The initial impression you communicate to an employer is regarded by many employers as a weak indication of what you will be like as an employee.

____ **12.** How effectively you present yourself in the interview will probably determine whether you get a job offer.

____ **13.** Being prepared for the interview is important because you have a limited amount of time to convince the interviewer why you should be hired.

____ **14.** Affirmative Action and Fair Employment programs enable employers to identify minority group candidates so they can increase their numbers of minority employees.

____ **15.** It is good business manners to write a letter expressing your appreciation for time spent during an interview and to inform the interviewer whether you are interested in the job.

Use a separate sheet of paper to rewrite the statements you marked false and make them true. Include the number of each statement you rewrite.

Taking Responsibility for Your Job Success

Chapter **10**

Attitude—The Great Communicator

You send messages to people every day. Some of your messages are positive; others are negative. Your attitude can be revealed by what you say (verbally), by your appearance, or by your actions.

Imagine that you are the manager of a large department store. You have the authority to hire, fire, promote, and give raises to employees. For each of the following situations, mark the type of attitude message the employee is sending you.

Attitude Message Sent by Employee	Positive or Negative?	Verbal, Action, or Appearance?	Mature or Immature?
Example: Has a firm handshake	Positive	Action	Mature
1. Wears dirty clothing to work			
2. Arrives early for work			
3. Breaks expensive glass merchandise and laughs			
4. Tells a coworker, "Do it yourself; it's not my job"			
5. Thanks a coworker for a suggestion			
6. Listens patiently to an obnoxious customer			
7. Arrives late for work at least once a week			
8. Insults a customer			
9. Uses incorrect grammar when speaking to customers			
10. Gives coworkers a helping hand whenever possible			
11. Is frequently absent from work with very weak excuses			
12. Wears clean, appropriate clothing to work			

If you were selecting an employee for promotion or were considering someone for a pay raise, which two positive attitude messages from the preceding list would be most important to you? Write their numbers and explain the reason for each decision.

Number:_____ Reason: _____

Number:_____ Reason: _____

What's Your Usual Attitude?

Your attitude is a reflection of your inner feelings. It influences your work, and your work influences your attitude. How would you feel about and respond to the following situations?

You are a salesperson in a clothing store. A customer yells at you because the dye in a shirt he purchased from you faded when he washed it. The customer slams the faded garment on your counter, demands his money back, and threatens to sue your store.

How does this make you feel? _____

What do you say or do? _____

_____

You are an airplane mechanic. The airplane you are working on is scheduled to fly in 12 more hours. You spent the first four hours of your shift finding an engine problem and acquiring the necessary parts. Your shift ends in four hours, and you will need about six hours to complete the repairs.

How does this make you feel? _____

What do you say or do? _____

_____

You are an accountant. It is Friday, and you are collecting information about production costs to help write a budget for your employer. You were told that the information would not be due for another week, but this afternoon your boss tells you that she needs it Monday morning. You will have to work all weekend to complete your assignment.

How does this make you feel? _____

What do you say or do? _____

_____

In which situation did you maintain the most positive attitude? Why was this situation easiest for you?

_____

_____

_____

In which situation were you least able to maintain a positive attitude? Why was this situation most difficult for you?

_____

_____

_____

As you consider future occupations, keep in mind that the first situation entails working with people, the second situation entails working with things (tools and machines), and the third situation entails working with data (information and numbers).

Rate Your Work Values

Consider the list of worker behaviors that follows. You might consider some of these behaviors to be very important and others to be less important. Use the following rating scale to rate each behavior from 1 to 5, according to your personal work values.

Rating Scale: 5 = Very important; 4 = Somewhat important; 3 = Of average importance; 2 = Not very important; 1 = Unimportant.

Work Behavior	Your Rating
Example: Always addresses a boss as "Sir" or "Ma'am"	3
Spends additional time when necessary to complete a work task	
Uses care in handling tools and equipment	
Leaves his or her work area and equipment in good condition	
Thinks before speaking and listens carefully	
Is cooperative with supervisors, coworkers, and customers	
Assumes responsibility for acquiring needed skills	
Consistently arrives at work on time	
Maintains a high level of personal cleanliness and grooming	
Responds to stress in a mature, appropriate manner	
Demonstrates an interest in learning new skills	

Total your score for the 10 worker behaviors. Write the total here:_____

Compare your total with the following guidelines.

Score	Guidelines for Understanding
50	Most employers would agree with you.
40–49	Your answers were thoughtful and positive. You have a good understanding of what employers expect.
30–39	Check the behaviors you rated lowest. Review "Section 2: Beginning a New Job" in Chapter 10.
5–29	Your score indicates a very unrealistic understanding of what employers expect from employees. Discuss your answers with a successful worker. Review "Section 2: Beginning a New Job" in Chapter 10.

Legitimate Absence or Not?

Imagine that you are the assistant manager of a large grocery store. You are responsible for hiring and training employees and operating the store efficiently. How would you handle the following situation?

You hired William three months ago as a part-time bagger. He works three hours each evening after school during the store's busiest time. When the cashier has to bag groceries, the checkout line slows, customers become angry, and business is lost. In fact, you must either pull another employee off of his or her job to bag groceries or do it yourself.

William is a very efficient worker, displays a pleasant attitude, and had perfect attendance for the first two months. However, he has phoned in sick each of the past three Thursdays. He always phones your office at about 11:30 a.m. When you phoned the school attendance office, a worker there informed you that William wasn't absent from school on the days he missed work. When you phoned William's home, his mother told you he was at work.

It is Friday evening, and William has just arrived at work. He was absent yesterday, and you know he attended school and wasn't home sick. You ask William to report to your office. You very calmly tell William everything you know about the situation and ask him for an explanation. Use the following lines to write William's explanation.

_____

_____

_____

1. Do you believe William's explanation? Why or why not?

_____

_____

2. What course of action will you take?

_____

_____

3. Will your course of action cause the store to operate more efficiently? If so, how? If not, why are you following this course of action?

_____

_____

_____

4. Will the other employees think you have treated William with fairness? How will your course of action influence your relations with the other workers?

_____

_____

_____

Finding the Right Words

Chapter 10 of your textbook contains numerous terms that employers and workers use. Recognizing and understanding these terms will help you make the important career decisions you will soon face.

Fill in the blank spaces using the vocabulary terms to complete the following sentences.

1. Workers demonstrate p _ s _ t _ v _ _ tt _ t _ d _ s when they are courteous, cooperative, and considerate with their coworkers and superiors.

2. C _ mp _ t _ nc _ is another word for "being capable."

3. People who help others project a desired image are called _ m _ g _ c _ ns _ lt _ nts.

4. Sch _ d _ l _ d br _ _ ks are rest periods that employers provide so employees can take time out from the workday to relax, have refreshments, handle personal needs, or socialize with coworkers.

5. A l _ g _ t _ m _ t _ _ bs _ nc _ occurs when an employee must miss work for a reason that is acceptable to the employer.

6. _ nt _ rd _ p _ nd _ nc _ occurs when you depend on a group and the group depends on you.

7. One rule of business _ t _ q _ _ tt _ is to be attentive during meetings.

8. Meetings or activities to acquaint you with the employer's purpose and organization are called j _ b _ r _ _ nt _ t _ _ n programs.

9. Tr _ _ n _ ng m _ n _ _ ls detail the use or repair of equipment or describe procedures to follow on the job.

10. S _ cc _ ss is a favorable result or a hoped-for ending.

11. All employers have a unique set of rules known as p _ l _ c _ _ s _ nd pr _ c _ d _ r _ s.

12. The level of enthusiasm displayed by workers in the workplace is called their m _ r _ l _.

13. The first few weeks and months on a new job make up an _ r _ _ nt _ t _ _ n p _ r _ _ d.

14. Your highest level of productivity is referred to as your f _ ll p _ t _ nt _ _ l.

15. A pr _ b _ t _ _ n _ ry p _ r _ _ d is a specific period of time in which you are expected to prove your ability to perform the job.

16. P _ rs _ n _ l _ pp _ _ r _ nc _ is an important factor in career success.

Checking Your Location

For each of the following statements, write **F** if the statement is more false than true. Write **T** if the statement is more true than false.

____ **1.** Attitudes affect the way people get along at home, at school, and at work.

____ **2.** Many attitudes are learned in early childhood.

____ **3.** After you learn to be interdependent, your next step is to become a member of society at the highest level: independence.

____ **4.** Attitudes toward work and personal responsibility start at school.

____ **5.** On a new job, you must learn the particular duties and responsibilities you were hired to perform, and your performance must meet your employer's expectations.

____ **6.** Motivation to succeed is frequently based on the need to survive, to obtain social approval, or to obtain self-respect.

____ **7.** Successful people know their values and have learned to listen to them. Another word for the values that help us make decisions is *conscience*.

____ **8.** After you have been hired, your supervisor and your closest coworkers will have considerable influence on your career success.

____ **9.** On the job, dress with enough fashion to be noticed.

____ **10.** On the job, your supervisor and coworkers will depend on you. Your absence could affect other workers' ability to proceed with their jobs.

____ **11.** Your employer will expect you to be ready to work at starting time, stay until quitting time, and take no more than the allotted time for lunch and other scheduled breaks.

____ **12.** Many of your employer's policies and procedures will be confusing. Using your own judgment will eliminate most confusing situations.

____ **13.** Much of your job success will depend on how well you follow your employer's policies and procedures.

____ **14.** Getting along well with others will help you enjoy your work, and your supervisor will appreciate your cooperative attitude.

Use a separate sheet of paper to rewrite the statements you marked false and make them true. Include the number of each statement you rewrite.

Making Progress on the Job

Chapter **11**

Fitting into the Corporate Culture

Understanding your employer's corporate culture will help you learn what personal behaviors and job performance are expected. Make an appointment to visit a local business workplace to observe its corporate culture. (A parent, friend, or neighbor can probably give you the name of a contact person in the organization in which he or she is employed.) Record the following information:

1. The name of the business you visited: _____

2. The product or service the business manufactures or provides: _____

3. Observe the type (style) and purpose of clothing worn by specific workers.

Occupation of worker: _____

Type and purpose of clothing:

_____

Occupation of worker: _____

Type and purpose of clothing:

_____

4. Observe the style (grammar) and purpose of verbal communication used by workers.

Occupation of worker: _____

Style and purpose of verbal communication:

_____

_____

Occupation of worker: _____

Style and purpose of verbal communication:

_____

_____

5. Observe the form and purpose of written communication used by workers.

Occupation of worker: _____

Form and purpose of written communication:

_____

_____

Occupation of worker: _____

Form and purpose of written communication:

_____

_____

6. Do the employees seem to get along with one another? _____

What specific employee behaviors did you observe that support your opinion?

_____

_____

_____

7. Based on your observations, describe the corporate culture of the organization you visited.

_____

_____

_____

8. Overall, would you fit in with the corporate culture of this employer? Explain your answer.

_____

_____

_____

Being Supervised

Imagine that today is your first day on the job and you are feeling nervous. Certain questions are going through your mind. What will your new boss expect? Will your job performance be acceptable? What will it be like to have a boss? It occurs to you that school and work are very similar. Having regular attendance, being on time, completing your assignments on schedule, getting along with coworkers, and following the supervisor's instructions are all part of being successful on the job. Write your response to each of the following work situations.

It is your first week on the job. Your new boss is giving you directions. She speaks very rapidly, and you are not sure what she expects you to do.

How do you handle the situation?

_____

_____

What impression do you expect your response to have on your boss?

_____

During your second week on the job, you arrive 20 minutes late to work one day because of unusually heavy traffic. Your boss gives you a lecture and a warning.

How do you handle the situation?

_____

_____

What impression do you expect your response to have on your boss?

_____

It is your third week on the job. You are doing household chores on your day off and plan to attend a movie with friends during the evening. The boss phones you at home. She is shorthanded and wants you to work this evening.

How do you handle the situation?

_____

_____

What impression do you expect your response to have on your boss?

_____

The boss calls you to her office during your fourth week on the job. She is upset because the project you are working on is two days late and still unfinished. In fact, you are doing most of the work, and your two coworkers are not doing their share. Both of your coworkers have more than 10 years of service.

How do you handle the situation?

_____

_____

What impression do you expect your response to have on your boss?

_____

Getting Along with Coworkers

Building positive relationships with coworkers is an important part of career success. Whether or not you like certain coworkers, you must interact with them on the job. Consider the students in your class as coworkers as you complete the following activity.

Describe a situation in which a person didn't agree with your position and it turned out that he or she was right and you were wrong.

_____

_____

What did you do when you discovered you were wrong?

_____

_____

Did your action strengthen or weaken your relationship with the other person?

_____

If you had it to do over again, how would you handle your behavior in this situation?

_____

_____

Describe a time when you started or repeated a rumor about someone or when another person started or repeated a rumor about you.

_____

_____

Were feelings or reputations injured by the rumor?

_____

Did you attempt to make the situation better? If so, how? If no, why not?

_____

_____

If you had it to do over again, how would you handle your behavior in this situation?

_____

_____

Describe a situation in which another person praised your work or behavior or did something for you to demonstrate his or her appreciation.

_____

_____

How did you respond? How did you feel?

_____

_____

Describe a situation when you praised another person's work or behavior or did something to demonstrate your appreciation.

_____

_____

How did the other person respond? How did he or she appear to feel?

_____

_____

Describe a situation in which someone asked you a question or interfered with a task you were performing that was clearly none of his or her business.

_____

_____

What feelings or emotions did you have as a result of the other person's interference?

_____

_____

How did you handle the situation?

_____

_____

Describe a situation in which another person was very late or didn't remember an important appointment with you.

_____

_____

How did the other person's behavior influence your feelings toward him or her?

_____

_____

If you were an employer, how would you handle the situation in which a worker makes excuses for failing to be on time or complete work projects on schedule?

_____

_____

Working Together

Review "Section 5: Understanding Labor Unions" in Chapter 11 of your textbook before beginning this activity. In each of the following cases, circle the letter of the option that you prefer most.

1. I prefer that my wages and hours of employment be established by

   a. Bargaining between a union (including myself and my coworkers) and my employer

   b. My employer

2. When a difference of opinion arises between workers and management, I would prefer

   a. To accept the opinion of an impartial third party

   b. To accept the decision of my employer or resign

3. When bargaining between my employer and union fails, and my coworkers vote to strike, I would prefer

   a. To strike until the employer agrees to an acceptable compromise

   b. To accept the employer's terms and continue working

In general, the **a** preferences represent the position of most union members, and the **b** preferences represent the position of most employers. Think about the reasons for your answers as you read the following case study.

Tracy Ewing recently completed her tech-prep program, earning an associate degree in electocardiograph technology. After a job search of several weeks, two health-care organizations offered her jobs. The jobs and the employers seem very similar, with one exception: The employees of one organization are represented by a union, and the employees of the other organization are not. Tracy has asked you to help her compare and evaluate the two job offers.

Would you advise Tracy to accept the job with the unionized or nonunion employer? Describe the reasons for your advice:

_____

_____

_____

_____

_____

_____

_____

_____

_____

_____

_____

_____

_____

Finding the Right Words

Chapter 11 of your textbook contains numerous terms that employers and workers use. Recognizing and understanding these terms will help you make the important career decisions you will soon face.

Unscramble the terms in column B and match them with the definitions in column A. (Some terms contain two words.)

Column A	Column B
Example: __a__ moving up in an organization	a. _____career advancement_____ rareec tadcanvemen
1. ___ differences of opinion over the interpretation of a labor contract	b. _____ tellivececo graingabin
2. ___ the lowest level of job experience	c. _____ meti gameteamnn
3. ___ the negotiating process between labor unions and employers	d. _____ ropecorat trueluc
4. ___ an organization that represents workers in negotiations with their employer	e. _____ vanriceseg
5. ___ a member of the supervisor's staff	f. _____ krow cithe
6. ___ planning ahead to make the best use of your time	g. _____ renty veell
7. ___ the thoughts, feelings, manners, and sense of good taste that each business or organization develops	h. _____ rabol snunio
8. ___ the idea that through hard work individuals can make their own success	i. _____ broadensuit
9. ___ workers who work as a group to identify and solve problems	j. _____ corksower
10. ___ people who work together and rely on one another to complete work assignments	k. _____ risetinyo
11. ___ the supervisor in a team management system	l. _____ meat saverdi
12. ___ the length of time spent with an employer	m. _____ ityaluq ricecl

Checking Your Location

For each of the following statements, write **F** if the statement is more false than true. Write **T** if the statement is more true than false.

____ **1.** Unless you have previous experience, your first job with an employer will probably be at the entry level.

____ **2.** What is acceptable in one work setting might not be acceptable in another.

____ **3.** In a large organization, your immediate supervisor will have little influence on your future progress.

____ **4.** Traditional control-oriented management produces the highest levels of productivity.

____ **5.** Your ability to get along with your supervisor depends a lot on your attitude toward criticism and authority.

____ **6.** Sooner or later, you will probably have a boss you don't like or one who doesn't like you. The best solution is to quit the job and find a better boss.

____ **7.** Most full-time employees spend more of their waking hours with coworkers than with family and friends.

____ **8.** Having lunch or taking your breaks with the workplace gossips is a good way to find out what is going on in the organization.

____ **9.** Finding humor in a bad situation makes it less stressful.

____ **10.** The best predictor of future performance is past performance.

____ **11.** If you become the supervisor of your former coworkers, personal relationships will change.

____ **12.** The purpose of the National Labor Relations Board is to administer, interpret, and enforce the National Labor Relations Act.

____ **13.** Where management has been receptive and where workers' interests have been adequately reflected, unions have increasingly shown a willingness to work with management for the overall success of the enterprise.

On a separate sheet of paper, rewrite the statements you marked false and make them true. Include the number of each statement you write.

Defining Roles, Rights, and Responsibilities

Chapter **12**

Self-Evaluation

Evaluators must be objective if they are to evaluate employees accurately. Be honest, objective, and accurate as you complete the following self-evaluation. Review each of the following situations. Then use the rating scale to rate how often you would probably respond in a certain way.

Rating Scale: 1 = Almost always; 2 = Usually; 3 = About half the time; 4 = Not usually; 5 = Almost never.

____ **1.** When I am with a group of friends and they ask for my opinion, I am able to speak clearly and present my views effectively.

____ **2.** When I am required to write information on a job application, a driver's license form, or other required applications or forms, my writing is neat and legible and presents information effectively.

____ **3.** When I take part in activities that require skill (sports, board games, musical performances, and so on) with my friends, I have the skills needed to be an effective participant.

____ **4.** When I am at home or involved with my friends, I am dependable and accurate in carrying out my responsibilities.

____ **5.** When I am involved in a disagreement with a friend or family member, I handle the situation in a calm, objective manner.

____ **6.** When I am involved in a group work activity with friends or family members, I am cooperative and open to suggestions from other members of the group.

____ **7.** When I belong to an athletic team, club, or other social organization, I have good attendance and show up on time for scheduled meetings or events.

____ **8.** When I am in a classroom and the teacher asks for my opinion, I am able to speak clearly and present my views effectively.

____ **9.** When I perform everyday written assignments at school, my writing is neat and legible and presents information effectively.

____ **10.** When I take part in major academic classes at school (English, math, science, social studies), I have the skills needed to be an effective participant.

____ **11.** When I am at school, I am dependable and accurate in completing my assignments and other responsibilities.

12. When I am involved in a disagreement with a teacher or a student I dislike, I handle the situation in a calm, objective manner.

13. When teachers make group assignments, I am cooperative and open to suggestions from other members of the group.

14. I have good attendance at school. I am seldom late for classes.

Each situation you rated yourself on represents a major area of concern for employers. Expect to be in similar job situations when you join the workforce.

Total your 14 scores and write the total here: ____

Scores will range from a possible low of 14 to a possible high of 70. The following table will help you interpret your self-evaluation.

Your Score	A Career Counselor's Interpretation of Your Score
14	Three strong possibilities exist: (1) You are exceptional, (2) you avoided a decision by rating each item with a 1, or (3) you have difficulty accepting your weaknesses.
15–20	Are you closer to a score of 14 or 21? Check the advice for both. Employers will appreciate several of your positive, mature responses. Review the situations in which you gave yourself a score of two or higher. Work to improve in these areas.
21	Employers will expect you to display positive attitudes and mature behaviors and to perform at an expected skill level "almost always." They will expect you to be on time, be cooperative, be dependable, and be able to perform the job tasks every day. Rethink the situation in which you rated yourself 2 or higher. Work to improve yourself in these areas.
22–27	Are you closer to a score of 21 or 28? Check the advice for both.
28	Your average response was a 2, "Usually," but this will not be good enough in the world of work. Review your ratings of 2 or higher. What can you do to improve?
29–41	Are you closer to a score of 28 or 42? Check the advice for both.
42	You react in a positive way and at an expected level about "half the time." If you owned a business, would you hire or keep a worker who followed instructions, showed up for work, was on time for work, and demonstrated adequate job skills only about half the time? Review "Section 1: Performance Appraisals" in Chapter 12 of your textbook.
43–70	Are you serious about your future career and lifestyle? Do you expect to qualify for postsecondary education and training? Do you plan to have high-paying, steady employment throughout your career? If your answer to these questions is yes, it's time for a major reality check. You still have time to prepare for career success. However, the clock is ticking, and the ball is in your court.

Where Is the Limit of Honesty?

One value or ethic that's important to most individuals and organizations is honesty—the belief in truth and justice. Some questionable actions of workers and employers will never appear in a newspaper headline, but many people would consider them to be dishonest. Consider the following case.

Leona needs to leave work 30 minutes early to keep a dental appointment. She asks Randy (a coworker) if he will punch out her time card at the regular quitting time. Randy agrees. At the close of the shift, the supervisor discovers Randy punching out two time cards. After a short meeting in the office, the supervisor gives Randy a warning and two weeks off work to think about it. When Leona reports to work the next day, the supervisor fires her. This was the second time Leona had left early without permission.

1. Would you consider Leona's behavior to be dishonest, unethical, or acceptable? (Choose one.) Explain the reasons for your answer.

_____

_____

2. Would you consider Randy's behavior to be dishonest, unethical or acceptable? (Choose one.) Explain the reasons for your answer.

_____

_____

3. Would you consider the supervisor's behavior to be dishonest, unethical, or acceptable? (Choose one.) Explain the reasons for your answer.

_____

_____

4. If you were the supervisor, how would you have handled the problem with Randy?

_____

_____

5. If you were the supervisor, how would you have handled the problem with Leona?

_____

_____

6. If you were Randy, what response would you have made when Leona asked you to punch out her time card?

_____

_____

7. If you were Leona, how would you have handled the need to leave work early?

_____

_____

Name_____ Class_____ Date_____

Is It a Violation of Your Legal Rights?

Congress has enacted many laws protecting the rights of workers that employers must follow. Many states offer additional protection. Consider the following situations.

Chris is the assistant manager of a large supermarket. He is paid a monthly salary. Based on a 40-hour week, his hourly wage is more than that of the workers he supervises. However, the workers receive a premium pay of one and a half times their regular rate for hours worked over 40, and Chris is expected to work extra hours without additional pay. As a result, Chris sometimes works longer hours than the workers he supervises and earns less.

1. Is Chris's employer violating his legal rights as a worker? _____

2. Which federal law covers this situation?

_____

3. What provision of the law covers this situation?

_____

_____

_____

4. If you were Chris, would you arrange a meeting with the store manager to discuss this situation? If so, what action would you expect from the manager? If not, why not?

_____

_____

_____

Paul graduated from a community college program with a machinist/machine technologist certificate. Although Paul is hearing-impaired, he graduated first in a class of 84 students. He applied for an entry-level machinist job with a large tool-and-die manufacturer. A week later, Paul received a rejection letter from the employment manager. The manager thanked Paul for considering his company for employment and congratulated him on his skills and high level of achievement. However, the manager felt that Paul's hearing impairment would be a safety hazard in the machine shop.

1. Is the employment manager violating Paul's legal rights as a worker? _____

2. Which federal law covers this situation?

_____

3. What provisions of the law covers this situation?

_____

_____

_____

_____

Fringes—What Are They Worth to You?

Because your fringe benefits are not received directly as wages, they are usually not subject to taxes. They are hidden income. However, employers are not legally required to provide most of the fringe benefits that workers receive.

Imagine that you are employed full-time and pay income taxes of 1 percent to the local government, 4 percent to the state government, and 20 percent to the federal government. Unfortunately, your employer doesn't provide medical insurance. The monthly premium for the basic medical insurance you have purchased is $75.

How much money must you earn each month to pay your medical insurance premium? _____

Imagine that you have changed jobs. One of the fringe benefits your new employer provides is a health insurance policy that is similar and in some ways better than yours. Your earnings on the new job are $100 per month more than your earnings on the previous job.

Has your actual spending power increased by $200 per month, decreased by $100 per month, or stayed the same?

_____

Consider the following fringe benefits offered by some employers. Then rank them in terms of their importance to you, with 1 being most important and 8 being least important.

____ Partially paid medical insurance (employer pays 70 percent)

____ Wellness program

____ Paid vacation plan

____ Parenting leave

____ Fully paid pension plan

____ Disability insurance plan

____ Excellent child-care program

____ Fully paid life insurance plan

What are your reasons for the number 1 selection?

_____

_____

What are your reasons for your number 8 selection?

_____

_____

Name_____ Class_____ Date_____

A Schedule That Works

Take a moment to think about your ideal job. Factors to consider include wages, job tasks, work environment, and of course, work schedule. A work schedule that fits your general lifestyle will increase your level of job satisfaction.

When you are at work, it is important to feel alert and ambitious. Would you describe yourself as a morning person or a night person?

_____

List your three favorite leisure activities. (Examples include camping, sports such as basketball or baseball, music, or hanging out with friends.) Then list the day of the week and the time of day that you prefer to be involved in each activity.

Leisure Activities	Day of Week	Time of Day

Imagine that it is 10 years from now. Consider whether you will be married, have children, own or rent a home, or be responsible for certain family members. List the four most important family and household responsibilities you expect to have. Then list the day of the week and the time of day you prefer or need to be involved with each responsibility.

Family and Household Responsibilities	Day of Week	Time of Day

How many of the activities and responsibilities on your lists would you prefer doing during the

Morning? ____   Afternoon? ____   Evening? ____   Night? ____

Now that you have reviewed your personal time priorities, which of the following work schedules would fit your planned lifestyle? (Choose one.)

____ A fixed day shift   ____ A split shift   ____ A fixed evening shift   ____ A swing shift

____ A fixed night shift

Review the days of the week in which the activities and responsibilities on your list occur. List the two days of the week that you would prefer to be off work.

1. _____

2. _____

Finding the Right Words

Chapter 12 of your textbook contains numerous terms that employers and workers use. Recognizing and understanding these terms will help you make the important career decisions you will soon face.

Unscramble the terms in column B, and match them with the definitions in column A. (Some terms contain two words.)

Column A	Column B
Example: _a_ rules that make monopolies illegal	a. ____antitrust laws____ tuntirast wasl
1. ___ the federal law that established a national social insurance program	b. _____ thesic
2. ___ a work schedule in which employees set their own hours of work	c. _____ timer ginrate
3. ___ leave taken by mothers or fathers when a child is born or adopted	d. _____ sailco riceyuts cat
4. ___ standards of conduct for what is believed to be right	e. _____ tixmeelf
5. ___ a formal, periodic, written evaluation of your job	f. _____ greatpinn veale
6. ___ Title VII of this 1964 law protects workers against discrimination	g. _____ citred nosuni
7. ___ one-day training courses offered by employers	h. _____ porkshows
8. ___ forms of compensation other than salary or wages	i. _____ tentincgno roekrw
9. ___ nonprofit banking services that employees may join	j. _____ liivc sightr cat
10. ___ a temporary, contractual, or leased employee	k. _____ efring finebset
11. ___ using knowledge obtained as a result of your position for personal gain	l. _____ dafur
12. ___ businesses with no competition	m. _____ rinised besua
13. ___ something said or done to deceive	n. _____ pimosenool
14. ___ reporting wasteful or dishonest company activities to the government	o. _____ nisenop slapn
15. ___ regular lifetime payments provided to employees on retirement	p. _____ shetilw-gliwbon
16. ___ agreement between competitors to establish specific price ranges for products or services	q. _____ ecirp nixfig

Checking Your Location

For each of the following statements, write **F** if the statement is more false than true. Write **T** if the statement is more true than false.

____ **1.** Employers have the right to evaluate the work performance of their employees.

____ **2.** The way information in a performance appraisal will be used is determined by the employer or, in the case of a union shop, by a contract between the workers and the employer.

____ **3.** It is not your supervisor's role to evaluate your performance; it is your responsibility to perform at or above minimum standards.

____ **4.** The Fair Labor Standards Act (FLSA) limits the hours of work for employees who are 16 years old or older.

____ **5.** The 1971 Fair Credit Reporting Act (FCRA) requires employers to tell rejected job applicants if they are denied a job based on credit information.

____ **6.** About 9 out of 10 workers, including household employees and the self-employed, are covered by Social Security.

____ **7.** After ethical standards are established and agreed on, all members or employees of the organization are expected to practice them.

____ **8.** Ethical behavior is a matter of personal values. Although points of view might vary, little harm can be traced to unethical behavior.

____ **9.** An employer has the right to take action against an employee for good cause.

____ **10.** Employers are required by law to provide a minimum package of fringe benefits for their workers.

____ **11.** Health maintenance organizations (HMOs) are expensive and provide a very limited range of health services.

____ **12.** Leave time is excused time away from work; it can be paid or unpaid.

On a separate sheet of paper, rewrite the statements you marked false and make them true. Include the number of each statement you write.

Managing Career Change and Growth

The Wise Old Owl

Imagine that you are the author of a career advice newspaper called *The Wise Old Owl*. What career advice would you offer the following workers?

Dear *Wise Old Owl*:

I graduated from high school four years ago and acquired a full-time job as a machine operator in a plastics molding factory. My car is paid for, and I have a small savings account. However, I would have trouble meeting all my bills if I didn't live with my parents. Many of my friends have just graduated from two-year colleges and already earn more money than I do. What should I do?

Disappointed in Atlanta

Dear Disappointed:

_____

_____

_____

_____

_____

_____

Dear *Wise Old Owl*:

I am a secretary working for the vice-president of a small factory. She is a very pleasant and considerate boss. I enjoy the work and feel that I have learned a great deal since I graduated from high school three years ago. The company seems to be doing very well, but I haven't received a pay increase for almost two years. I hate to quit my job, but I need to earn more money. What should I do?

Need More Money in Boston

Dear Need More:

_____

_____

_____

_____

_____

_____

What Is Career Success?

What will it take to make you feel successful? The success you feel in your future role as a worker won't exist separately from your life outside the job. Review the following career success factors. Using the following rating scale, rate them in order of importance from 1 to 5, according to your career ambitions.

Rating Scale: 5 = Very important to me; 4 = Somewhat important to me; 3 = Of average importance to me; 2 = Not very important to me; 1 = Unimportant to me.

____ **Job status:** Having rank and prestige within the organization

____ **Job security:** Feeling confident about job stability

____ **Advancement opportunities:** Knowing that you have a good chance for promotion within the organization

____ **Potential income:** Being certain that you will have enough money to pay for your lifestyle

____ **Work environment:** The quality and type of surroundings (indoor or outdoor, new or old)

____ **Education and training:** The amount of education and training you achieve (high school, technical school, two-year degree, four-year degree, graduate school)

____ **Work schedule:** The required shift and hours of work or the flexibility to establish your own hours of work

____ **Job responsibilities:** Being responsible for the job performance of others or having others responsible for your job performance (supervising or being supervised)

____ **Leisure time:** Having enough paid vacation time, holidays, and weekly hours away from the job to enjoy your personal lifestyle

Write the titles of the three success factors that are most important to you.

1._____ 2._____ 3._____

What occupations are you presently considering for your future career?

_____

Will the occupation you are presently considering satisfy the three success factors that are most important to you? If so, describe how the occupation will satisfy each factor. If not, what other occupations could you consider that would satisfy your important success factors?

Success factor 1: _____

_____

_____

Success factor 2: _____

_____

_____

Success factor 3: _____

_____

_____

The Process of Resigning

Don't make the mistake of being angry and creating bad feelings when you resign from a job. At some future date, you may want a reference. Consider the case of Carl.

Carl is starting his third week as a driver-salesperson for the Sunrise Bakery Company. It is 5:30 a.m., and Carl is preparing to load his delivery van. It will be another 10 hours before he returns to the bakery, sweeps out the inside of his van, and goes home. Carl is thinking about the long hours, low pay, and exhausting workload. The supervisor looks in the back of Carl's van. "Sweep it out," she says. "Don't load your van until it's spotless." Carl looks his supervisor in the eye and replies, "You sweep it out. I quit."

1. Is Carl a responsible employee? What evidence can you show to support your position?

_____

_____

2. Imagine that it is 15 years later, and Carl needs a job. The supervisor and all of Carl's coworkers have left the Sunrise Bakery Company. Do you think a new supervisor would hire Carl? Why or why not?

_____

_____

3. If you were Carl, how would you have handled this situation? Be specific.

_____

_____

Good business etiquette requires you to give a two-week notice to your employer before you resign.

1. Why is an advance notice important to the employer?

_____

_____

2. How could giving advance notice be important to you?

_____

_____

Can you think of a time when you started something important and then quit?

1. What did you start?_____

2. What were your reasons for starting?

_____

_____

3. What were your reasons for quitting?

_____

_____

4. Did you act in a responsible, mature manner in this situation? What did you do?

_____

_____

Losing Your Job

Millions of U.S. workers are laid off or fired from their jobs every year. After they are over the shock, disbelief, and anger, most of them make a new beginning. Every unemployed worker's situation is different.

Imagine that you are an employment counselor asked for advice in the situations described as follows. Use the following list of options (A to D) to make your recommendations. You can suggest more than one option. In each case, describe the reasons for your advice.

Options for Unemployed Workers

A   Seek employment locally in the same occupation.

B   Seek employment in a different region of the country.

C   Seek education and training to update your skills in the same occupation.

D   Seek personal career counseling before you attempt to become reemployed.

Charles is a diesel engine mechanic with six years of experience. He was fired today for having excessive absences.

Recommended options: _____

Reasons for your recommendations:

_____

_____

_____

Bret was laid off today from his position as a general office worker. He has a high school education and one year of experience. Bret works in a large urban area. Employment is very good in the region. Bret's employer has installed a computer system and no longer needs workers to perform general tasks such as typing and filing.

Recommended options: _____

Reasons for your recommendations:

_____

_____

_____

Tricia, a legal administrative assistant, was laid off today. She is a tech-prep graduate with an associate degree. Her job was in the small town in which she grew up. Tricia's employer retired, and the other lawyer has a legal assistant. Tricia loved her career. She will receive six months of severance pay and an excellent letter of recommendation.

Recommended options: _____

Reasons for your recommendations:

_____

_____

_____

Finding the Right Words

Chapter 13 of your textbook contains numerous terms that employers and workers use. Recognizing and understanding these terms will help you make the important career decision you will soon face. Fill in the blank spaces in the vocabulary terms to complete the following sentences.

1. A s _ l _ r _ is employee compensation that is calculated weekly, biweekly, monthly, or annually.

2. _ a _ e _ are employee compensation calculated hourly.

3. When a worker is not employed and is looking for work, he or she is _ n _ m _ l _ y _ d.

4. _ e t _ a _ is the amount of earnings that an employee receives after deductions are taken.

5. Compensation at greater-than-regular rates, such as overtime pay, is referred to as pr _ m _ _ m _ a _.

6. Incentive compensation, in which a percentage of company profits is distributed to the employees involved in producing those profits, is called _ ro _ i _ s _ a _ i _ g.

7. _ o _ mi _ s _ _ n _ are compensation to salespeople based on a predetermined percentage of the salesperson's sales value.

8. D _ _ c _ a _ g _ of an employee means dismissal from employment.

9. M _ ri _ i _ _ r _ _ ses are increases in workers' pay rates, usually given on the basis of efficiency or performance.

10. A _ a _ o _ f is an involuntary separation of an employee from an employer for a temporary or indefinite period, through no fault of the employee.

11. _ ne _ p _ _ y _ en _ i _ s _ _ a _ ce is a joint federal-state program that pays a weekly benefit to eligible workers when they are involuntarily unemployed.

12. _ o _ _ e _ u _ i _ y is protection against loss of employment and earnings.

13. P _ _ k s _ i _ is a common term used by workers to describe a notice of termination.

14. A law passed Congress in 1985 to help certain terminated employees buy group insurance for themselves and their families is commonly referred to as _ O _ _ A.

15. The part of your paycheck that provides you with a source of cash is called d _ r _ c _ c _ mp _ ns _ t _ _ n.

Checking Your Location

For each of the following statements, write **F** if the statement is more false than true. Write **T** if the statement is more true than false.

____ **1.** The career path you select will entail numerous personal and occupational changes.

____ **2.** As you change your role from student to employee, the importance you attach to different aspects of having a job will change.

____ **3.** Your definition of a satisfying job is usually formed during your high school years and changes very little during your career.

____ **4.** Family, friends, and social and professional support are all interrelated with job satisfaction in a worker's overall feeling of success.

____ **5.** Jobs have numerous characteristics that make them desirable or undesirable to workers.

____ **6.** Geographic location has little to do with wage rates.

____ **7.** The type of job you have and the policy of your company will have a lot to do with when you will receive a pay raise.

____ **8.** Millions of Americans change jobs each year. Many choose to change; others have no choice.

____ **9.** If the first job you select is a poor choice, you have made a total waste of your time and education.

____ **10.** Employers are required by law to provide a minimum package of fringe benefits for their workers.

____ **11.** If you are asked to submit a letter of resignation, don't be afraid to describe problems created by the organization or your supervisor. Top management will appreciate your information.

____ **12.** Whatever the cause of unemployment, those who are most highly skilled and trained are most likely to be reemployed.

____ **13.** A general rule of law states that "no employer shall discharge an employee without good cause."

____ **14.** Organizations are not consistent in how they lay off or terminate employees.

____ **15.** In most firings, the employee to be released knows in advance or at least has some suggestion that termination is coming.

On a separate sheet of paper, rewrite the statements you marked false and make them true. Include the number of each statement you write.

Adapting to a Changing Workplace

Chapter **14**

The Past—The Future

List one advance in technology that has taken place during the past 50 years in each of the following occupations. Describe how the advance has affected the occupation. The first one is done for you.

Occupation	Technological Advance	Effect of the Technology on the Occupation
Accountant	Spreadsheet programs	Bookkeeping can be completed more quickly
Musician		
Nurse		
Bank teller		
Engineer		
Physicist		
Dentist		
Pharmacist		
Journalist		
Aircraft pilot		
Cashier		
Retail salesperson		
Secretary		
Police officer		
Chef		
Farmer		
Mechanic		
Carpenter		
Assembly-line worker		
Truck driver		

Overall, have advances in technology been beneficial for these workers? Explain your answer.

_____

_____

_____

Issues: Sexual Harassment, Pregnancy, and Contingent Employment

Ashley is the only female in the junior welding program at Eastern Vocational School. The instructor, Mr. Smith, frequently makes jokes about any mistake she makes in the shop. The male students use Mr. Smith's jokes to tease Ashley. One student in particular makes repeated sexual comments. When Ashley complained to Mr. Smith, she was told she had better get used to it if she planned to work with men.

1. Is anyone guilty of sexual harassment in this class? If so, whom?

_____

2. How would you handle this problem if you were Ashley?

_____

_____

3. What would you do if you were the instructor?

_____

_____

4. How would you react if you were a male student in the class and felt that Ashley was being harassed?

_____

_____

_____

Temporary disability insurance (TDI) laws provide partial salary replacement for nonwork-related disabilities, including childbirth and pregnancy-related conditions. Should all states have these kinds of laws? Explain your answer.

_____

_____

_____

_____

The contingency (leased) labor force is growing faster than the rest of the labor force. However, only one-third of contingency workers receive health benefits. Should there be a national health-care program to make up for this benefit? If so, how should it be paid for? If not, why not?

_____

_____

_____

_____

Making the Labor Market Fair for All Workers

More women, minorities, and immigrants will participate in the labor force in the years ahead than ever before. These groups have often been relegated to low-paying, low-status occupations because of long-standing stereotypes and prejudices and because of limited educational and life experiences. As a result, they have not reaped the full benefits of career fulfillment.

The U.S. Equal Employment Opportunity Commission regularly collects information from companies to find out what kinds of jobs different groups of people have. The following table shows some of this information. In this table (which is based on information collected in 2002), occupations are grouped into nine main categories: officials/managers, professionals (jobs requiring a college degree), technicians (jobs requiring vocational training or two-year degree), sales, clerical, craft workers (jobs requiring extensive training, including mechanics and those in building trades), operatives (workers who operate machinery and have some training), laborers (unskilled work with little training), and service workers. Note that these numbers do not include people who work for the government or people who work in businesses with fewer than 100 employees.

Read the table and the following facts and answer the questions:

- Men make up about 52.5 percent of the workforce, and women make up about 47.5 percent of the workforce.

- Minorities currently make up about 30 percent of the workforce. In this group, 13.9 percent are black, 10.9 percent are Hispanic, 4.5 percent are Asian, and .7 percent are Native American. Growth in the Hispanic and Asian communities due to immigration and other factors will increase the number of workers from these groups in the near future.

Key: WM = white men; WW = white women; BM = black men; BW = black women; HM = Hispanic men; HW = Hispanic women; AM = Asian men; AW = Asian women; NAW = Native American men; NAW = Native American women.

Percentage of Workers in Occupational Groups by Race and Gender

	WM	WW	BM	BW	HM	HW	AM	AW	NAM	NAW
Managers	16.4	9.4	6.0	4.4	5.4	4.0	10.3	6.1	8.5	5.4
Professionals	17.5	21.0	6.3	10.2	5.2	7.4	32.9	31.4	10.7	12.2
Technicians	6.6	6.3	4.6	5.8	4.0	3.7	9.0	6.9	6.4	7.1
Salespeople	11.0	14.8	9.6	13.2	8.3	14.4	7.6	10.5	10.1	17.7
Clerical workers	5.0	24.1	7.6	25.6	5.7	22.0	6.7	17.3	7.3	22.4
Craft workers	13.6	2.1	9.4	1.9	11.1	2.2	6.0	2.1	15.2	2.5
Operatives	16.0	6.2	23.1	9.6	21.0	10.6	11.7	8.5	19.6	9.0
Laborers	7.0	4.2	14.9	6.7	20.9	14.1	6.3	5.3	11.6	7.1
Service workers	6.9	11.9	18.5	22.7	18.4	21.5	9.5	11.9	10.5	16.5

1. According to the table, which occupational group has the lowest percentage of female workers?

   _____

2. What do you think is the reason for the low number of women in this occupational group?

   _____

   _____

3. Operatives work in manufacturing jobs. According to the numbers in the table, which groups of people would be most affected by a large decrease in the number of manufacturing jobs?

   _____

   _____

4. Which group of people has the lowest percentage of service workers? _____

5. The service industry is projected to be a big source of economic growth in the coming years. What do you think keeps the people in question 4 from being service workers?

   _____

   _____

6. Managerial, professional, and technical jobs require the most education and tend to pay more than jobs in the other occupational groups. Which groups of people have the lowest percentage of workers in these occupational groups?

   _____

   _____

   _____

   _____

7. What is preventing the groups of people in question 6 from working in these higher-paying, skilled jobs?

   _____

   _____

8. How big of a problem do you think discrimination in the workplace is? What do you think should be done to handle this problem?

   _____

   _____

   _____

9. What can employers do to increase workers' appreciation for diversity in the workplace?

   _____

   _____

   _____

Men's Roles—Women's Roles

Men and women can be discouraged from pursuing certain careers because of stereotypes about the work role. They often do not consider a particular career because they simply do not know anyone like them in that career.

In the following list of occupations, write an **M** next to the occupations you usually associate with men, a **W** next to those you usually associate with women, and a **B** next to those you usually associate with both sexes.

____ Physician	____ Pharmacologist
____ Chemist	____ Lab technician
____ Engineer	____ Auto mechanic
____ Secretary	____ Accountant
____ Lawyer	____ Firefighter
____ Cashier	____ Dietician
____ Teacher	____ Computer scientist
____ Banker	____ Skilled trades apprentice
____ Nurse	____ Technologist
____ Architect	____ Executive

1. Is your father's occupation a traditional one for men? _____

2. Is your mother's occupation a traditional one for women? _____

3. Why do you believe women enter occupations you indicated with a **W**?

_____

_____

_____

4. Why do you believe men enter occupations you indicated with a **M**?

_____

_____

_____

The following chart lists characteristics frequently associated with men or women. In the Me column, check off those qualities that you believe describe you. In the Men/Women/Both column, write an **M** next to the qualities you most often associate with men, a **W** next to those you most often associate with women, and a **B** next to those you most often associate with both genders. In the last column, check off the characteristics you think are representative of a person with a career requiring advanced math or science skills.

Qualities Associated with Men or Women

Characteristic	Me	Men/Women/Both	Characteristics for Careers Requiring Advanced Math/Science Skills
Analytical			
Self-confident			
Abstract thinker			
Intelligent			
Loner			
Well-read			
Independent			
Decision maker			
Scientific			
Creative			
Patient			
Observant			
Studious			
Logical			
Ambitious			
Patient			
Responsible			

1. How many characteristics did you think applied mostly to men? _____

To women? _____

2. How many characteristics that described you did you also think applied mostly to men? _____

To women? _____

3. How many characteristics describing yourself are associated with a nontraditional career for your gender?

_____

4. Do you see any pattern in your responses?

_____

_____

Take Note: All the characteristics listed are generally associated with a career using advanced math and science skills.

Job Mobility and Adapting to Change

In less than 100 years, we have gone from a nation of farmers to a highly technical and mobile society. Today, less than 3 percent of Americans are farmers, and 75 percent of us now live on less than 3 percent of the land. Jobs are changing rapidly due to the reorganization of companies, technological changes, and an expanding international economy. Workers of the future can expect at least three to four career changes requiring retraining during their working life.

1. Why is it important to be aware of job trends when planning your future career?

_____

_____

2. What are two occupations you are now considering for your future career?

Occupation 1: _____

Occupation 2: _____

3. What technological changes do you predict for these careers by the year 2020?

_____

_____

4. What social, political, and economic changes can you imagine that would alter the future growth of these occupations?

_____

_____

_____

_____

Your lifestyle would be affected by the location of your future career. The house you live in, the car you drive, the activities you do for enjoyment, the type of food you prefer, the friends you have, the family you are a part of, and the way you spend your income are all part of your lifestyle. Describe three lifestyle needs that will be important to you as an adult.

1. Where do you plan to live? _____

2. Who will live with you? _____

3. What recreational activities will you enjoy?

_____

Consider the reaction of the Catalano family to a recent move. Mr. Catalano took a new job that required relocating the family from Fort Worth, Texas, to Little Rock, Arkansas. Mr. Catalano loves his new job. He has made a lot of friends at the plant and is excited about remodeling an older home overlooking the Arkansas River. Cheryl Catalano is 16 years old. She misses her friends in Texas, she's unhappy with her new school, and she feels sad most of the time. Angelo Catalano is 12 years old. He made the basketball team at his new school, he loves fishing on the Arkansas River, and he feels great most of the time. Mrs. Catalano doesn't say a lot about the move to Arkansas. She misses her family in Texas, but she really likes her new job at Dillard's corporate headquarters.

1. How do you think things would be for you if you were put in a similar situation this year?

_____

_____

2. How do you think you would adapt if you were making the move for a career opportunity?

_____

_____

3. What advice would you offer to Cheryl?

_____

_____

4. What advice would you offer Mrs. Catalano?

_____

_____

At some point in your career, you might need to move to a new job or take a transfer. You might become unemployed and unable to find local employment. You might need to seek employment opportunities in another geographic area, or you might simply wish to move to a different area. This kind of lifestyle change causes emotional highs and lows for most people. Some people cope better than others.

1. What would you be willing to give up for a job you really wanted? Check all that apply.

Close family ties _____   Favorite activities _____   Friends _____   Educational plans _____

Familiar restaurants and shopping areas _____   Place of worship _____

2. How would you react to these changes in lifestyle?

_____

_____

3. Does the occupation you are most seriously considering fit your lifestyle goals? Explain your answer.

_____

_____

_____

Finding the Right Words

Complete the word-find puzzle by finding and circling the vocabulary terms you learned in this chapter. (They are listed as follows.) The words appear horizontally, vertically, and diagonally.

attributes

deregulation

glass ceiling

maternity leave

nontraditional occupations

offshore

outsourcing

production flexibility

sexual harassment

telecommuting

unprecedented

urban area

```
E R I R E W P Q L Y U R P F H Q N F J L C M L T N
V B M H Y P Q R N Y T F D M N S J E X G X I O O G
A H H G D B Q H Y A U U P E P Q Z C G Q G U N B L
E S Q B G H Q Y C R H B Z N R G U A V M X T L E A
L V A Y P S E T U B I R T T A E G M U O R D Z R S
Y D J J N D R V N N N Y F U M N G Z Q A F E Y O S
T Y T I L I B I X E L F N O I T C U D O R P U H C
I W Q C W S X M H M M K X T Q V T I L D L T G S E
N C H Q D I J L W Z G S U N N O T Y I A S D V F I
R X Q B P M I U C Y J M S O M I B P N O T U A F L
E J Q O N P U U W O M Y F A O H T R U Q N I S O I
T X S Y P B Y L S O D U Z N R F K R C F I Y O Y N
A H P Z L A N W C D L I A R E A C D C B K A F N G
M L I B A L B E S U C L O E V I H Y L O P F G O V
A E P E F J L Z Z B O O T F N G K L Y N S X A U S
T E H C U E Y W D C P X U G U J R N A X I E K M J
C Q R V T G V N C I T P Q C G X R G I U J Z B N Z
K B C A B F Z U N P R E C E D E N T E D X L Q U O
G Y O F N O P J O R V S H J M B T B P K T E B W B
O J U X S A I B Y A D L L A E O T K A C B A S D K
Q T K C T D B B N Y I K W F W B H A R J R C V W E
R Z A I I T J R Y O P U M A F E Q O P C C C S U Y
Y D O A Z R O Z U V G V I O C G N S R X S A I J J
C N E T O U O U J A H J I A S G Q L L Y A F W Z G
S Z N H S O X Z L C K H C Q U T K X K P W P G P P
```

Checking Your Location

For each of the following statements, write **F** if the statement is more false than true. Write **T** if the statement is more true than false.

____ **1.** Employment in the goods-producing sector of the economy is projected to increase greatly by the year 2012.

____ **2.** During World War II, women's earnings nearly equaled the average for men.

____ **3.** The feminist movement grew during the 1960s and 1970s as women were encouraged to seek a larger role in the labor market.

____ **4.** The opportunities for women in nontraditional occupations have increased significantly in the last 50 years.

____ **5.** The job of the EEOC is to protect workers from discrimination based on age, gender, race, color, national origin, religion, or disability.

____ **6.** U.S. companies can sometimes lower costs by hiring workers in India or Hong Kong to do data-entry work.

____ **7.** International job opportunities are greatest for those employees who speak more than one language.

____ **8.** Employers rarely include contingent employees in benefit programs such as health insurance, paid leave, or pensions.

____ **9.** Workers aged 55 to 64 are becoming the fastest-growing age group in the U.S. workforce.

____ **10.** Service-producing organizations continue to be the major source of economic growth.

____ **11.** Technology eliminates inefficient jobs and creates new jobs to replace them.

____ **12.** Workers on the West Coast and the East Coast generally have higher earnings than workers in the rest of the country.

____ **13.** Hiring contingent workers is more expensive than maintaining permanent workers.

On a separate sheet of paper, rewrite the statements you marked false and make them true. Include the number of each statement you write.

Connecting Economics and Work

Chapter 15

The United States—A Global Production System

Review "Section 1: Production and Service Systems" in Chapter 15 of your textbook before beginning this activity.

The production of consumer goods creates profits for employers and jobs for workers. List four consumer goods that you purchased during the past six months.

_____

_____

_____

_____

Cross out the consumer good you could most easily give up, and circle the consumer good you need the most. Why do you need this particular consumer good?

_____

_____

Name one consumer good that many families purchase today that was uncommon when your parents were your age.

_____

_____

How has the widespread use of this consumer good affected the average American's lifestyle?

_____

_____

_____

What occupations were created, increased in number, or were eliminated because of this consumer good?

_____

_____

_____

Industrial products are goods that are produced for and sold to other producers. List one industrial product used to manufacture each of the following:

Tires _____   Automobiles _____

Clothing _____   Donuts _____

Windows _____   Trash bags _____

The United States—A Global Service System

Review "Section 1: Production and Service Systems" in Chapter 15 of your textbook before beginning this activity.

The provision of consumer services for businesses and consumers creates profits for employers and jobs for workers. List four services that your family purchased during the past six months.

_____

_____

_____

_____

Cross out the service your family could most easily give up, and circle the service your family needs the most. If the service you circled were no longer available, how would it affect your everyday family life?

_____

_____

Name one service that many families purchase today that was uncommon when your parents were your age.

_____

_____

How has the widespread use of this service affected the average American's lifestyle?

_____

_____

What occupations were created, increased in number, or were eliminated because of this service?

_____

_____

_____

Industrial services are services that are produced for and sold to other businesses. List one industrial service that would be used by each of the following:

Gasoline service station _____

Hospital _____

Restaurant _____

Stock Ownership—Fuel for the Economy's Furnace

Whether you own 1 share or 1,000 shares, stock ownership makes you part owner of a business. In both good times and bad times, investors purchase shares of stock with hopes of making a profit. Although many people think of stockholders (owners of stock) as being wealthy, the majority are ordinary people. Depending on the type of stock they own, stockholders are entitled to a certain percentage of the profits and are permitted to vote on certain corporate matters.

Most investors—whether they are individuals with a few hundred dollars to invest or large institutions with millions—use securities sales representatives when buying or selling stocks. Securities and financial services sales representatives hold more than 200,000 jobs. Most sales representatives work for a small number of large firms with main offices in big cities (especially in New York) and approximately 25,000 branch offices in other areas.

Imagine that you are a securities and financial services sales representative for a large brokerage firm. Research the financial section of your daily newspaper or another newspaper, such as the *Wall Street Journal* or *USA Today*, for lists of businesses that buy and sell on the New York Stock Exchange.

- You are to invest $10,000 for a client.

- You have three weeks to work with this investment.

- You can purchase any number of stocks you choose in blocks of 100 or more.

- You must charge your client $30 for each stock transaction (purchase or sale).

- You are limited to 10 purchase transactions and 10 sales transactions, using the daily close price.

- Record all your transactions on charts A and B.

Chart A: Record of Stock Purchases

Date of Stock Purchase	Name of Stock	Number of Shares Purchased	Price Per Share	Brokerage Fee ($30)	Total Cost of Stock Plus Brokerage Fee

Chart B: Record of Stock Sales

Date of Stock Sale	Name of Stock	Number of Shares Sold	Price Per Share	Brokerage Fee ($30)	Total Amount of Sale Minus Brokerage Fee

What is the difference between the purchase of the stocks you selected and the price you sold them for? (Note whether the price is up [+] or down [–] from the price you originally paid for each stock.)

Stock 1 _____ Stock 2 _____ Stock 3 _____ Stock 4 _____

Stock 5 _____ Stock 6 _____ Stock 7 _____ Stock 8 _____

Stock 9 _____ Stock 10 _____

At the end of three weeks, how much did you earn in brokerage fees? (The brokerage fee is charged to pay your commission and salary and the company's costs for doing business.) _____

How much did your client's account earn or lose during this three-week period?

Profit _____ Loss _____

Production, Quality, and Price

Review "Section 5: Technology and Change" in Chapter 15 of your textbook before beginning this activity.

Technology has changed the way we work. When workers are more productive, more goods and services are available at lower prices. Consider the case of Gordon Lee.

Gordon enjoyed making wooden furniture as a hobby. His specialty was a rocking chair. Several friends and neighbors admired Gordon's work and asked him to build rocking chairs for them. When a local furniture store offered to sell his chairs, Gordon decided to quit his job at the Legion Hall and build chairs full-time.

Working with hand tools in his garage, it takes Gordon three days to build one chair. He has orders for all the chairs he can build at $150 per chair. Recently, the owner of a furniture store in a nearby city saw one of Gordon's chairs at a friend's house. She has offered to buy six chairs per week at a price of $125 each. Gordon's business is doing very well, but he has a serious problem with productivity. If he can't keep up with the demand for his goods (chairs), he will begin to lose business.

1. What effect would you expect the decision to hire one or more workers to have on the quality and production of Gordon's chairs?

_____

_____

_____

2. What effect would you expect the decision to use power tools, such as a table saw and lathe, to have on the quality and production of Gordon's chairs?

_____

_____

_____

3. If you were Gordon, what steps would you take to increase production and maintain the high quality of the chairs you produce?

_____

_____

_____

_____

4. What course of action could Gordon follow to lower the price of his chairs and still make a satisfactory profit?

_____

_____

_____

_____

Changes in the Auto Industry

The U.S. automobile industry has undergone tremendous change since the late 1970s. Once the world's dominant motor vehicle producers, U.S. automakers faced increasingly fierce competition from foreign manufacturers during the 1980s. As one of the U.S. economy's largest employers, the auto industry affects the job prospects of hundreds of thousands of workers. Its lack of sustained employment growth during the 1980s had a negative impact on the U.S. economy.

Until the late 1970s, the American automobile market had remained fairly consistent throughout most of the twentieth century. The "Big Three" U.S. automakers—General Motors, Ford, and Chrysler—dominated the market. In 1946, worldwide output of automobiles amounted to 3.9 million units, with the United States producing 3.1 million, or 80 percent of the total. Japan produced 15,000 autos that year. By 1990, Japanese firms (both Japan- and U.S.-based) had captured 33 percent of all U.S. car sales, European firms had 5 percent, and Korean firms had 2 percent. Between 1979 and 1989, America's motor vehicles and equipment industry experienced a net loss of 105,000 jobs.

1. More than 100,000 American auto-related jobs were lost in 10 years due to sales of Japanese cars. What reaction would you expect from our world trading partners if the U.S. government simply refused to allow Japanese cars to be sold in the United States?

    _____

    _____

    _____

    _____

2. How can the United States or any other nation in the global economy react to foreign competition without losing jobs or angering global trading partners?

    _____

    _____

    _____

    _____

3. If one industry, such as the auto industry, loses jobs because of foreign trade but other industries create new jobs, how do we transfer workers from the declining industry to the new jobs? What if workers lack the necessary skills for the new jobs?

    _____

    _____

    _____

    _____

Finding the Right Words

Chapter 15 of your textbook contains numerous terms that employers and workers use. Recognizing and understanding these terms will help you make the important career decisions you will soon face. Fill in the blank spaces in the vocabulary terms to complete the following sentences.

1. E _ o _ _ mi _ s is the social science concerned with the way a society uses its productive resources to fulfill the needs and wants of each member.

2. A _ ca _ cit _ exists when people have limited resources compared with their wants.

3. _ e _ _ i _ es are tasks that other people or machines do that cannot be physically weighed or measured.

4. _ nd _ str _ _ l _ r _ d _ ct _ are goods that are produced for and sold to other producers.

5. A _ a _ ke _ comprises people or organizations that purchase a particular good or service.

6. Resources or benefits that a business gives up to produce a particular product or provide a particular service are known as the _ pp _ rt _ n _ ty c _ s _.

7. Natural resources, labor, capital, and management are examples of l _ m _ t _ d _ e _ ou _ _ e _.

8. An e _ o _ o _ i _ s _ s _ e _ is the method a society uses to determine how it will use and distribute available resources.

9. In a f r _ _ _ nt _ rpr _ s _ _ y _ t _ m, people can own the means of production, can have the freedom to use them as they see fit, and can freely create and operate businesses.

10. _ ro _ i _ is the money left over after all expenses are paid.

11. D _ m _ _ d is the willingness of consumers to buy goods or services at a certain price in the marketplace.

12. A person or group that buys or uses goods or services to satisfy personal needs and wants is a c _ ns _ m _ r.

13. The total value of goods and services that a nation produces for the marketplace during a specific period of time, usually a single year, is known as the g _ o _ s d _ m _ _ t _ c p _ _ d _ c _.

Checking Your Location

For each of the following statements, write **F** if the statement is more false than true. Write **T** if the statement is more true than false.

____ **1.** The word *economics* comes from the ancient Greek word *oikonomikos*, which means "the management of a household."

____ **2.** For most purposes, the terms *capitalist system*, *market system*, and *free enterprise system* have the same meaning.

____ **3.** Government regulations can limit certain areas of free choice, private ownership, competition between businesses, or the right to make unlimited margins of profit.

____ **4.** Every time a new idea is turned into a product or service and a business is formed to produce the product or provide the service, workers are laid off, jobs are eliminated, and profits are restricted.

____ **5.** Profit is the major motivator of every business.

____ **6.** Services are usually more difficult to distribute than goods.

____ **7.** Consumers give little thought to prices if the product is high quality and satisfies a need or a want; producers want to sell the highest possible volume of their products or services without worrying about profits.

____ **8.** When a business obtains complete control of the supply or demand of a good or service, it becomes a monopoly.

____ **9.** Early settlers on the American frontier had little need for money.

____ **10.** The Federal Deposit Insurance Corporation (FDIC) protects banks against losses on real estate mortgages.

____ **11.** During periods of good times and business peaks, economic activity reaches its highest point in the business cycle.

____ **12.** Workers are protected, in part, from bad times by unemployment benefits.

____ **13.** When the average price of goods and services decreases over a prolonged period of time, the economy is in a period of inflation.

____ **14.** As systems of communication and production technology change at a dizzying pace, the skill requirements for jobs become more sophisticated.

____ **15.** Ninety-five percent of the customers buying goods in the world economy live outside the United States.

On a separate sheet of paper, rewrite the statements you marked false and make them true. Include the number of each statement you write.

Starting a Business

Chapter 16

Follow Your Hobbies to Entrepreneurship

In Chapter 16 of your textbook, you learned that our free enterprise economic system encourages people to become entrepreneurs. Many entrepreneurs began by turning their hobbies and other activities into money-making opportunities.

Match the hobbies or activities in column B with the entrepreneurs in column A that are most related.

Column A	Column B
___ Owner of an auto repair shop	**a.** Having pets and caring for them
___ Owner of a photography studio	**b.** Raising flowers and having a garden
___ Owner of a lawn and garden store	**c.** Being active in sports activities
___ Owner of a health spa	**d.** Riding and repairing bikes; later driving and repairing automobiles
___ Owner of a kennel	**e.** Taking photographs of family and friends

1. What are your two favorite hobbies or activities?

_____

2. What two skills have you developed from these hobbies or activities?

_____

_____

3. Name one business that uses these skills. _____

4. How would an entrepreneur use these skills?

_____

5. What hobbies do you suppose the following entrepreneurs enjoyed?

Elvis Presley (musician) _____

Bill Gates (founder of Microsoft) _____

Liz Claiborne (Liz Claiborne Fashions) _____

Walt Disney (Walt Disney Productions) _____

6. Name one new product or service that you want in your community. _____

7. As an entrepreneur, how would you go about making this product or service available in your community?

_____

_____

Entrepreneurship—Is It for You?

Outgoing, upbeat, enthusiastic, positive-thinking risk takers are good candidates for entrepreneurship. From each group of three statements below, select the one that is most like you. Circle the statements you select.

1. **a.** I like to play a competitive sport.

   b. I like to watch TV.

   c. I like to go to parties.

2. **a.** I enjoy adventurous activities.

   b. I enjoy safe activities.

   c. I enjoy routine activities.

3. **a.** I prefer to organize work tasks my own way.

   b. I prefer to help others to organize tasks.

   c. I prefer to have work tasks organized for me.

4. **a.** I like being responsible for my actions.

   b. I like sharing responsibility with others.

   c. I like not being responsible for things.

5. **a.** I know I can succeed at a task.

   b. I am usually able to succeed.

   c. I frequently don't succeed.

6. **a.** I like new ways to solve problems.

   b. I am cautious when solving problems.

   c. I like proven answers.

7. **a.** I enjoy organizing people for a purpose.

   b. I enjoy being a useful member of a group.

   c. I don't care for groups of people.

8. **a.** I don't quit until the problem is solved.

   b. I do it right the first time.

   c. I don't waste time on problems.

9. **a.** I like to find new ways to do things.

   b. I like to be careful about new ways of doing things.

   c. I like to do things by using proven methods.

10. **a.** I frequently take risks.

    b. I seldom take risks.

    c. I am always sure of what I do.

11. a. I become impatient with delays.

    b. I accept delays without anger.

    c. I am not at all concerned with delays.

12. a. I prefer to plan and make my plan work.

    b. I do good work without planning things.

    c. I prefer to follow plans that are given to me.

13. a. I use my time efficiently.

    b. I spend a lot of time just enjoying whatever I'm doing.

    c. I'm seldom concerned about time.

14. a. I refuse to quit until I succeed.

    b. If it doesn't work, I try something else.

    c. Often, success isn't worth the trouble it requires.

15. a. I like to learn and improve from my failures.

    b. I like to be cautious and not fail.

    c. Most things don't make a difference to me.

16. a. I would enjoy producing a new product.

    b. I would enjoy producing a proven, quality product.

    c. The type of product is unimportant.

Count the total number of **a**, **b**, and **c** statements you circled.

Total **a** statements: _____   Total **b** statements: _____   Total **c** statements: _____

Number of *a* Responses	Similarity to an Entrepreneur
11–16	You have very strong entrepreneurial characteristics.
8–10	You have a greater-than-average interest in entrepreneurship.
5–7	You have an average interest in entrepreneurship.
0–4	You have very little similarity to an entrepreneur.

Review the **a** statements that you circled, and give examples of times when you demonstrated these entrepreneurial characteristics.

_____

_____

_____

_____

_____

_____

_____

A Franchise Is Best for Some Entrepreneurs

Statistics indicate that 9 out of 10 franchises succeed during their first year of business. Select a franchise business that interests you and contact the owner of that business. It can be a McDonalds, H & R Block, UniGlobe Travel, Jiffy Lube, or any franchise that you frequent. (For additional names of franchises, review Gale Research's *Worldwide Franchise Directory*.) If the owner is busy, explain the purpose of your call and ask if you can make an appointment to interview the owner at a time that is convenient for the owner. Ask the following questions in your interview.

Name of entrepreneur: _____

Name of business: _____

1. Why did you choose to be associated with this company and its products and services?

_____

_____

_____

2. What kind of training did you receive to operate this franchise? (Did your training include selling, merchandising, advertising, and bookkeeping?)

_____

_____

_____

_____

3. What manuals and sales and marketing aids are available?

_____

_____

4. Did the franchisor check to see whether you have the background experience and financial ability to succeed in the franchise?

_____

5. Does the franchisor provide continuing assistance? If so, what kind of assistance?

_____

_____

_____

6. What were the franchise fees and the initial investment royalties?

_____

_____

7. Did the franchisor offer to help finance the franchise?_____

8. What are your rights and obligations according to your contract, including any restrictions on business activities if you leave the franchise?

_____

_____

_____

_____

_____

9. What inventory, equipment, and working capital did you need to open the franchise?

_____

_____

_____

10. Do you have exclusive rights to a certain territory?

_____

_____

11. What do you like about having this franchise? What don't you like?

_____

_____

_____

_____

_____

_____

12. Would you buy the franchise again? _____

Why or why not?_____

_____

_____

_____

_____

Name_____ Class_____ Date_____

Select a Business and
Develop a Plan for Its Success

When people think about running a business, they frequently think about working for or with people. What about businesses in which you spend most of your time working with facts or machines? An entrepreneur might have a business working with people, facts, or things.

Look back at your answers to the "Data, People, or Things?" worksheet in Chapter 2. Record your totals here:

People: _____ Data: _____ Things: _____

Review the yellow pages of your telephone book. Find four businesses that match your people, data, and things interests. (Some promising fields in the years ahead are energy, environment, hazardous waste handling, robotics, health care, child care, and elder care.)

_____   _____

_____   _____

Circle the business you would be most interested in owning.

1. Imagine that you are starting a business of the type you have circled. What goods or services will you offer?

_____

2. Who will be your target market? (Include age, gender, and interests.)

_____

3. What are the positive aspects of this business for you? What are the negative aspects?

_____

_____

_____

4. What form of business will you have (sole proprietorship, partnership, franchise, corporation)?

_____

5. What are the advantages of this form of business to you?

_____

_____

6. What are the disadvantages of this form of business to you?

_____

_____

7. What special licenses or permits will you need to operate legally?

_____

8. What will you name your business?_____

9. Where will you locate your business? Why?

_____

_____

10. What will make your business different from and better than your competition?

_____

_____

11. How will you promote your business so that it is profitable?

_____

_____

12. What prices will you charge? _____

13. What will you need to learn to be successful in this business?

_____

_____

14. What resources can you locate to help start and maintain your business?

_____

_____

15. What supplies, tools, furniture, special equipment, and inventory will you need to start your business?

_____

_____

16. How many employees will you need?_____

17. What are their job titles?

_____

_____

18. What will your business hours be? Open:_____ Close:_____

19. What days of the week will you be open? _____

20. What is one reason why your business might fail?

_____

_____

21. What entrepreneurial characteristics do you have that will make you succeed?

_____

_____

On a separate sheet of paper, write a newspaper advertisement to announce the opening of your business. Consider the image you want to project and the specific customers you are trying to reach.

Profit or Loss—Income and Expenses

The amount of income received from a business transaction minus the expenses of conducting the transaction equals the profit. If the total cost of the transaction is greater than the amount taken in, there is a loss.

Remember Erica from Chapter 16? She started the Pied Piper Day-Care Center. She will hire extra employees in the summer for children who are in grades 1 through 3. Calculate Erica's daily and weekly profit or loss for the two weeks described as follows. Use a separate piece of paper for your calculations.

Formula: Total money received – cost = profit

        Cost – total money received = loss

Date	Total Receipts	Wages	Rent	Equipment and Supplies	Profit	Loss
Monday, 12/2	$780	$500	$000	$185		
Tuesday, 12/3	$1,100	$500	$000	$45		
Wednesday, 12/4	$912	$500	$000	$38		
Thursday, 12/5	$912	$375	$000	$55		
Friday, 12/6	$580	$500	$550	$135		
Profit/Loss Totals						
Weekly Total						

Date	Total Receipts	Wages	Rent	Equipment and Supplies	Profit	Loss
Monday, 6/17	$2,200	$850	$000	$295		
Tuesday, 6/18	$1,800	$850	$000	$383		
Wednesday, 6/19	$2,400	$990	$000	$225		
Thursday, 6/20	$2,275	$990	$000	$265		
Friday, 6/21	$1,800	$1,075	$550	$445		
Profit/Loss Totals						
Weekly Total						

Figure the monthly profit or loss for each of the following businesses. First, figure the gross profit by subtracting the cost of goods sold from the net sales. Second, figure the net profit or loss by subtracting the operating expenses from the gross profit.

Company	Sales	Goods Sold	Gross Profit	Expenses	Net Profit	Net Loss
J&R Books	$4,790	$2,440		$1,240		
Stolz Personnel	$240,650	$144,067		$76,800		
Waterloo Transmission	$184,400	$136,800		$65,200		

Piles of Paperwork

The Fair Labor Standards Act (FLSA) requires employers to keep records on wages, hours, and other items. Remember Erica and her Pied Piper Day-Care Center? Her sister Lindsay became her business partner, and the business became very successful. Describe three types of employees that would be needed to operate the Pied Piper Day-Care Center. Include their job titles and work tasks.

_____

_____

_____

The employees of Erica's day-care center work an eight-hour day with time and a half for hours over eight per day. Use the following payroll worksheet to calculate the wages the business must pay this week.

Employee	Hours per Day M T W T F	Hourly Rate	Overtime Rate	Regular Wages	Overtime Wages	Total Wages
Barbara Tate	8 12 8 12 8	$6.00	$9.00			
Janet Simms	8 12 8 12 8	$6.20	$9.30			
Alonzo Adams	8 8 8 8 8	$9.50	$14.25			
Trisha Wilson	8 0 8 0 7	$6.00	$9.00			
Mack Johnson	8 8 8 8 10	$15.00	$22.50			
Arnold Smith	8 8 8 8 8	$6.00	$9.00			
Traci Garcia	8 8 8 8 8	$7.00	$10.50			
Akeesha Brown	8 8 8 8 8	$7.00	$10.50			
Total wages for the week						

Note that Trisha Wilson didn't come to work on Tuesday and Thursday. She was an hour late on Friday. What effect did this have on the weekly payroll?

_____

_____

_____

_____

Which employee would you expect to be the most skilled? What makes you think so?

_____

Finding the Right Words

Chapter 16 of your textbook contains numerous terms that employers and workers use. Recognizing and understanding these terms will help you make the important career decisions you will soon face. Unscramble the vocabulary words and then write them in the blank lines to complete the following sentences.

1. PENTRENERERUS _____ are people who have ideas, develop plans, and take action to pursue moneymaking opportunities.

2. LESO SPOTRIREPPORIH When the same person is both the owner and a worker, the type of business ownership is a _____.

3. TRAPOORICON You can become part owner of a _____ by buying one or more shares of stock.

4. SHICREANF When you buy a _____, you are able to use the name, logo, and business methods of an established company.

5. GRETTA KARMET To identify your _____, you need to research the people who are likely to buy your product or service.

6. HONOLTIGGIMN _____ is a way for beginning entrepreneurs to earn money while starting their businesses.

7. NETRUVE PACILAT Money earmarked for investment in new businesses is called _____.

8. BELACAN THEES The _____ summarizes what a business owns and what it owes.

9. MEPRIT Local government authorities charge a small fee to issue a _____ that allows a business to operate.

10. HACS WOFL In order to survive, a business must have a healthy _____.

11. FOTRIP-NAD-SLOS TENATTEMS A _____ includes information on sales, direct expenses, indirect expenses, and income.

12. RANELEG GRELED The principal book of accounts for a business is known as the _____.

13. STASES Fixed _____ are items such as land and equipment.

14. SIBILITAIEL Amounts owed to suppliers are considered to be current _____.

Name_____ **Class**_____ **Date**_____

Checking Your Location

For each of the following statements, write **F** if the statement is more false than true. Write **T** if the statement is more true than false.

_____ **1.** Entrepreneurs see business ownership as the most promising path to financial success, independence, and true job satisfaction.

_____ **2.** As long as you have a good product or service, the location of your business doesn't really matter.

_____ **3.** Most successful entrepreneurs earn better-than-average wages, and some become wealthy.

_____ **4.** According to the Small Business Association (SBA), most small businesses fail within one year.

_____ **5.** Most small business entrepreneurs acquire business capital by taking out personal loans.

_____ **6.** Successful entrepreneurs rely on luck and street smarts to help them develop their businesses while they run them.

_____ **7.** Most small gas stations, barber shops, restaurants, video stores, and campgrounds are sole proprietorships.

_____ **8.** Like an individual person, a corporation can sue or be sued in a court of law.

_____ **9.** All franchisors are required by law to provide a Uniform Franchise Offering Circular to the Federal Trade Commission.

_____ **10.** Financial institutions rarely require entrepreneurs to provide them with a written business plan before they will consider making a loan.

_____ **11.** Whether large, small, new, or well-established, sooner or later every business has problems, and the owner needs help.

_____ **12.** Most new enterprises lose money for several months or longer.

_____ **13.** Venture capitalists usually require the business owner to sell them 50 to 90 percent of ownership of the new business in return for the capital.

_____ **14.** Only large businesses must have an employer identification number to complete tax forms and other required government information forms during the life of a business.

_____ **15.** Business owners can deduct legal business expenses from their gross income to arrive at their taxable income.

On a separate sheet of paper, rewrite the statements you marked false and make them true. Include the number of each statement you write.

Managing Your Income

Chapter 17

Your Paycheck

Look at the sample pay stub shown here; then answer the questions that follow.

Name: Debi R. Mukherjee	Social Security No. 000-25-1411		Check No. : 0046271		
Pay period: 9/15/06 - 9/30/06					
Earnings	This Pay Period	Year to Date	Deductions	This Pay Period	Year to Date
Salary	1,154.25	26,547.75	Federal tax	142.61	3,279.92
Earnings			State tax	35.06	806.27
Hourly rate			City tax	23.09	530.96
Hours paid			FICA	125.02	4,270.80
Overtime rate			Pension	18.00	342.00
O.T. hrs. paid			Bonds		
Sales amount	480.00	9,500.000	United Way	5.00	90.0
Commission %	6		Health ins.		
			Dues		175.00
			Total Deductions	348.78	
	Gross Pay	1,634.25	Net Pay	1,285.47	
Illness Unpaid	Family Illness	Jury Duty	Vacation	Sick Leave Days Accum.	
	2	2	5	63	

1. What are the dates for this pay period? _____

2. What is the amount of Debi's gross pay for this pay period? _____

3. How much was taken out for the United Way?_____ For federal taxes?_____
   For city tax?_____

4. What is the amount of Debi's take-home pay? _____

5. Debi was paid for five vacation days. How much was this benefit worth to Debi if her annual salary is $46,535?_____

6. If Debi earns a 6 percent commission on sales of chemicals, what would her commission be on sales of $75,400?_____ On sales of $876.00?_____

7. Your Social Security number is used to track your earnings while you're working and to track your benefits when you're receiving Social Security. How much was deducted from Debi's pay this period for Social Security/FICA? _____

The W-2 Tax Form

Your employer will withhold (take out) taxes from your paycheck during the year and will deposit them in a federal bank. The amount your employer deducts is determined by how many dependents you tell your employer you have when you fill out your W-4 form. By the end of the year, you should have paid all or almost all of the income tax due on your yearly income.

Soon after the end of the calendar year in which you are employed, your employer will send you a W-2 form. This form shows how much you earned and how much income tax, Social Security, and Medicare was withheld from your earnings during the preceding year. Your withholding probably won't match your tax exactly. So when you report your income and figure your tax return for the year, you will usually have underpaid or overpaid your tax. If you owe money for taxes, you pay the balance due when you file your income tax return after the end of the year. If you paid too much, the IRS will send you a refund check after you file your return.

a Control number 001		OMB No. 1545-0008	Safe, accurate, FAST! Use IRS e-file	Visit the IRS website at www.irs.gov/efile.

b Employer identification number (EIN) 00-00001	1 Wages, tips, other compensation 18,900.00	2 Federal income tax withheld 2,839.00
c Employer's name, address, and ZIP code **CRS Sailing School** **2001 Dolphin Way** **Seaside, HI 00111**	3 Social security wages 18,900.00	4 Social security tax withheld 1,171.18
	5 Medicare wages and tips 274.05	6 Medicare tax withheld 274.05
	7 Social security tips	8 Allocated tips
d Employee's social security number 080-01-0404	9 Advance EIC payment	10 Dependent care benefits
e Employee's first name and initial Last name **Lindsay M. Millard** **700 Oceanview Drive** **Seaside, HI 00111**	11 Nonqualified plans	12a See instructions for box 12
	13 Statutory employee Retirement plan Third-party sick pay	12b
	14 Other	12c
		12d
f Employee's address and ZIP code		

15 State Employer's state ID number HI	XXX	16 State wages, tips, etc.	17 State income tax	18 Local wages, tips, etc.	19 Local income tax	20 Locality name

Form **W-2** Wage and Tax Statement   **2005**   Department of the Treasury—Internal Revenue Service

Copy B—To Be Filed With Employee's FEDERAL Tax Return.
This information is being furnished to the Internal Revenue Service.

Examine the sample W-2 form, and then answer the questions that follow.

1. How much did Lindsay earn during the tax year? _____

2. Who is her employer? _____

3. How much was withheld for federal income taxes? _____

4. How much was withheld for Social Security? _____

5. How much was withheld for Medicare? _____

6. What is Lindsay's Social Security number? _____

Take Note: If your Form W-2 shows an incorrect Social Security number or name, notify your employer or the form-issuing agent as soon as possible to make sure your earnings are credited to your Social Security record.

Filing Your Income Tax—(Form 1040EZ)

Note that this is not an official IRS Form 1040EZ and is to be used only for educational purposes.

Name and Address: Print your name, address, and Social Security number. For this activity, assume that you are single, have no dependents, and that no one can claim you for a dependent.

Presidential Election Campaign Fund: If you want to contribute to this fund, check the "yes" box. If you do not, check the "no" box. Checking "yes" does not change your tax or reduce your refund.

Report Your Income: In line 1, enter the total wages from the sample W-2 form in the preceding "The W-2 Tax Form" worksheet. In line 2, enter taxable interest. Assume that you earned $220 interest on your savings account. In line 3, assume you did not have any unemployment compensation. Enter -0-. For line 4, add lines 1, 2, and 3. This is your *adjusted gross income.*

Standard Deduction: In line 5, you must check yes or no. As an independent, single adult, you check no. Next, enter $7,950. In Line 6, subtract Line 5 from Line 4. If Line 5 is larger than Line 4, enter -0-. This is your *taxable income.*

Payments and Tax: For line 7, enter the federal income tax withheld from box 2 of your Form(s) W-2. For line 8a, assume that you are not eligible for earned income credit. Enter -0-. For line 8b, assume that you are not eligible for nontaxable combat pay. Enter -0-.

For line 9, add lines 7 and 8a; these are your *total payments.* Line 10: Use the amount on line 6 to find your tax on the table below. Enter your tax on this line.

If your 1040EZ taxable income (line 6) is

At least	But less than	Your tax is
10,900	10,950	1,281
10,950	11,000	1,289
11,000	11,050	1,296
11,050	11,100	1,304
11,100	11,150	1,311
11,150	11,200	1,319
11,200	11,250	1,326
11,250	11,300	1,334
11,300	11,350	1,341
11,350	11,400	1,349

For line 11a: If line 9 is larger than line 10, subtract line 10 from line 9. This is your refund. Enter the amount here. For line 11b and 11c, assume that you are not depositing a refund directly to your bank. Leave blank. For line 12: If line 10 is larger than line 9, subtract line 9 from line 10. Enter the amount you owe here.

Third Party Designee: Assume that you are taking charge of your own taxes. Leave blank.

Sign here: Take time to check all your math and be sure that data is properly entered before you sign.

Paid Preparer's Use Only: Assume that you are taking charge of your own taxes. Leave blank.

Form **1040EZ**

Department of the Treasury—Internal Revenue Service

Income Tax Return for Single and Joint Filers With No Dependents (99)

OMB No. 1545-0675

Label

(See page 11.)

Use the IRS label.

Otherwise, please print or type.

L
A
B
E
L

H
E
R
E

Your first name and initial | Last name

Your social security number

If a joint return, spouse's first name and initial | Last name

Spouse's social security number

Home address (number and street). If you have a P.O. box, see page 11. | Apt. no.

▲ **Important!** ▲
You **must** enter your SSN(s) above.

City, town or post office, state, and ZIP code. If you have a foreign address, see page 11.

Presidential Election Campaign (page 11) ▶

Note. Checking "Yes" will not change your tax or reduce your refund.
Do you, or your spouse if a joint return, want $3 to go to this fund? . . . . . . ▶

You Spouse
☐ Yes ☐ No ☐ Yes ☐ No

Income

Attach Form(s) W-2 here.
Enclose, but do not attach, any payment.

1 Wages, salaries, and tips. This should be shown in box 1 of your Form(s) W-2. Attach your Form(s) W-2. | 1

2 Taxable interest. If the total is over $1,500, you cannot use Form 1040EZ. | 2

3 Unemployment compensation and Alaska Permanent Fund dividends (see page 13). | 3

4 Add lines 1, 2, and 3. This is your **adjusted gross income.** | 4

Note. You **must** check Yes or No.

5 Can your parents (or someone else) claim you on their return?
Yes. Enter amount from ☐ worksheet on back.
No. If **single**, enter $7,950. If **married filing jointly**, enter $15,900. See back for explanation. | 5

6 Subtract line 5 from line 4. If line 5 is larger than line 4, enter -0-. This is your **taxable income.** ▶ | 6

Payments and tax

7 Federal income tax withheld from box 2 of your Form(s) W-2. | 7

8a **Earned income credit (EIC).** | 8a

b Nontaxable combat pay election. | 8b

9 Add lines 7 and 8a. These are your **total payments.** ▶ | 9

10 **Tax.** Use the amount on **line 6 above** to find your tax in the tax table on pages 24–32 of the booklet. Then, enter the tax from the table on this line. | 10

Refund

Have it directly deposited! See page 18 and fill in 11b, 11c, and 11d.

11a If line 9 is larger than line 10, subtract line 10 from line 9. This is your **refund.** ▶ | 11a

▶ b Routing number | ▶ c Type: ☐ Checking ☐ Savings

▶ d Account number

Amount you owe

12 If line 10 is larger than line 9, subtract line 9 from line 10. This is the **amount you owe.** For details on how to pay, see page 19. ▶ | 12

Third party designee

Do you want to allow another person to discuss this return with the IRS (see page 19)? ☐ **Yes.** Complete the following. ☐ **No**

Designee's name ▶ | Phone no. ▶ ( ) | Personal identification number (PIN)

Sign here

Joint return? See page 11.

Keep a copy for your records.

Under penalties of perjury, I declare that I have examined this return, and to the best of my knowledge and belief, it is true, correct, and accurately lists all amounts and sources of income I received during the tax year. Declaration of preparer (other than the taxpayer) is based on all information of which the preparer has any knowledge.

Your signature | Date | Your occupation | Daytime phone number ( )

Spouse's signature. If a joint return, **both** must sign. | Date | Spouse's occupation

Paid preparer's use only

Preparer's signature ▶ | Date | Check if self-employed ☐ | Preparer's SSN or PTIN

Firm's name (or yours if self-employed), address, and ZIP code ▶ | EIN | Phone no. ( )

For Disclosure, Privacy Act, and Paperwork Reduction Act Notice, see page 23. | Cat. No. 11329W | Form **1040EZ**

Checking Accounts

In this activity, you will learn how to keep accurate records of a checking account. Start by filling out the following checking account deposit slip for Cristina Almez. Cristina's paycheck totals $343.85. Keep $40.00 in cash for Cristina, and deposit the rest into her checking account. The date is September 24.

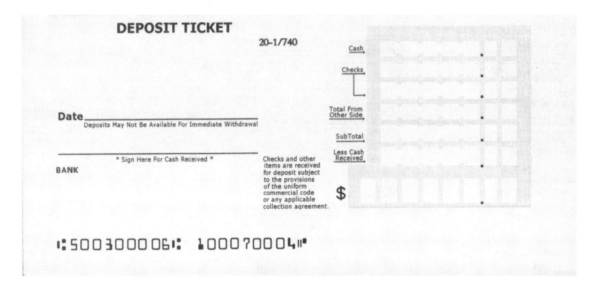

Make out the following check to Sunrise Gardens Apartments in the amount of $425.00 to pay for Cristina's rent. The date is September 25.

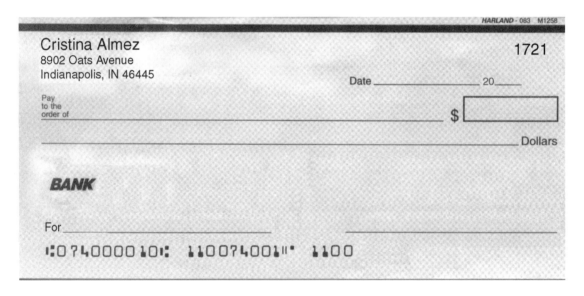

© JIST Works: Duplication Prohibited

On September 27, Cristina wrote a check (number 1722) to Lindsay's Trend Setter Shop for $39.63 for a sweater. On September 28, Cristina mailed a check (number 1723) for her monthly electric bill to the Midwest Electric Company. The check was for $63.75. Bring Cristina's check register up to date by entering a starting balance of $494.05 and recording the checking account deposit she made on September 24 and the checks she wrote to Sunrise Gardens Apartments, Lindsay's Trend Setter Shop, and Midwest Electric Company. Include the bank charge of $.35 for each check written.

NUMBER	DATE	DESCRIPTION OF TRANSACTION	PAYMENT/DEBIT (-)	CODE*	FEE (-)	DEPOSIT/CREDIT (+)	$ BALANCE
			$		$	$	

SUPPLEMENTAL CHECKING OR SAVINGS REGISTER

Balance the check register. (Add the amount of the deposits and subtract the amount of the checks written to figure the balance.) What is the balance in this account?

_____

How often should you balance your check register?_____

At regular intervals, the bank sends Cristina a bank statement. When she receives her bank statement, she puts her canceled checks in order by number; then she goes through the canceled checks one by one to check her records against the bank's record. The following checks were returned: numbers 1721, and 1723. Check them off in Cristina's check register in the correct box.

Which check or checks were not returned?_____

Cristina's deposit on 9/24/06 was recorded. Check this off on her check register.

According to the bank, what is Cristina's final balance? _____

Key to Success: Look at the back of a bank statement. Most bank statements have a printed format to assist you in balancing your account. Ask a family member whether you can help balance his or her account.

Savings Accounts

Your savings can be used for future purchases, education, or retirement. Regular savings is an important part of wise money management.

Write each of the following entries in the correct column of the following passbook savings account.

- On May 7, you made a deposit into savings of $125.
- On May 15, you made a deposit into savings of $66.
- On May 21, you made a withdrawal from savings of $98.
- On May 30, you made a withdrawal from savings of $50.
- On June 7, you made a withdrawal from savings of $75.
- On June 18, you made a deposit into savings of $100.
- On June 22, you made a deposit into savings of $96.
- On June 30, you made a deposit into savings of $25.

Figure the new balance after each entry. Then figure the interest on this account at the end of each month. Assume that the account earns 5 percent interest per year, compounded monthly (.05 x monthly balance ÷ 12 = monthly interest). Interest will be credited May 30 and June 30.

Date	Withdrawal	Deposit	Credited	Interest Balance
April 30				$430.00
June 30				

Develop a Successful Budget

Before you declare your independence and decide to make it on your own, you will need a realistic financial game plan: a budget. A budget will help you gain a sense of financial confidence and control. A budget will show you how much is coming in and how much is being paid out. The money coming in must be more than the money being paid out, or else you'll be in debt.

In this activity, assume that you are living on your own and have a job that pays $3,200 per month. With this income, establish a realistic budget by using the following categories.

	Monthly Estimate	Yearly Estimate		Monthly Estimate	Yearly Estimate
Income			**Relatively Fixed Expenses**		
Wages/salary (after taxes)	_____	_____	Food (at home, at restaurants)	_____	_____
Bonuses/commissions	_____	_____	Utilities (phone, fuel, trash, electricity)	_____	_____
Interest on savings	_____	_____	Transportation (fuel, bus, car repairs, parking)	_____	_____
Dividends on investments	_____	_____			
Other	_____	_____	Child care	_____	_____
Set-Asides			**Variable Expenses**		
Savings accounts, investments	_____	_____	Clothing	_____	_____
Emergency fund	_____	_____	Household repairs	_____	_____
Education (tuition, books)	_____	_____	Dry cleaning	_____	_____
Fixed Expenses			Health care (doctors, dentist, other)	_____	_____
Insurance (life, health, car, property, rental)	_____	_____	Entertainment (vacations and recreation)	_____	_____
Property taxes	_____	_____	Gifts/contributions	_____	_____
Rent or mortgage payment	_____	_____	Personal care (haircuts, etc.)	_____	_____
Loan payments, debt (car, student loans)	_____	_____	Other	_____	_____
Summary of Income			**Summary of Expenses**		
Total income (after tax deductions)	_____	_____	Total set-asides	_____	_____
Total savings and investments	_____	_____	Total fixed expenses	_____	_____
Total funds available each month	_____	_____	Total relatively fixed expenses	_____	_____
			Total variable expenses	_____	_____
			Total expenses	_____	_____
			Difference between available funds and expenses	_____	_____

List the six most expensive things you have to pay for when you are living on your own.

_____   _____

_____   _____

_____   _____

1. How well does your budget cover your expenses?

_____

2. Which two of the expenses listed will be most difficult to meet? Why?

_____

_____

3. Which six of the expenses listed are the most important to you?

_____   _____

_____   _____

_____   _____

4. Which six of the items listed would you be willing to give up first?

_____   _____

_____   _____

_____   _____

5. What is the least amount you must earn, after taxes, to live on your own? _____

Imagine that you want to have a new car and an apartment, but you can budget for only one at this time. Your wants exceed your resources. Use the rational decision-making plan described in Chapter 4 to make a decision.

Analyze the alternatives:

_____

_____

Check each alternative against personal attitudes, values, and culture:

_____

_____

Make the decision: _____

What is the opportunity cost of your decision? _____

What values influenced your decision?

_____

_____

How much consumer credit can you afford? (Consumer credit is short-term debt with a payback term of five years or less. It does not include a home mortgage.) This will be one of the key questions for managing your credit obligations. As a quick estimate, some financial advisers recommend limiting your consumer credit use to 15 to 20 percent of your current take-home pay.

In the credit capacity analysis that follows, use information from the budget you just completed. Write the amount of your take-home pay ($1,600) in (a). Write the amount of your total monthly expenses in (b). Subtract (b) from (a) and write the result in (c).

(a) Total take-home pay $_____

(b) Total expenses $_____

(c) Balance for credit, savings, etc. $_____

Income that exceeds expenses can be used for savings, additional spending, or credit repayments. If your expenses exceed $3,200, the balance is negative. This means that additional credit obligations should be avoided, and you should rework your budget so that it balances. How did you do?

Financial advisers recommend limiting your consumer credit use to 15 to 20 percent of your current take-home pay. The credit signal light is when your consumer credit use exceeds 15 percent. This is a signal to let you know that you should not make any more credit purchases until you lower your consumer debt. Use information from your budget to decide whether you have reached your limit on consumer debt.

Total take-home pay: _____

Total consumer debt owed (excluding rent/home mortgage): _____

15 percent of take-home pay:_____

Is the amount of consumer debt owed in your budget more than 15 percent of your take-home pay?

_____

If your answer is yes, you should reduce your debt before buying anything else on credit.

Finding the Right Words

Complete the word-find puzzle by finding and circling the vocabulary terms you learned in this chapter. (They are listed as follows.) The words appear horizontally, vertically, and diagonally.

bank statement	credit capacity	interest
bounced check	credit history	open-ended credit
budget	creditors	piecework
canceled check	deductions	savings account
certificate of deposit	deposit slip	sound financial management
check	electronic funds transfer	taxes
check register	endorsement	
compound interest	gross earnings	

```
K S M O R K F A T Y M B I Q L D J V J F S E E T
C O C R E D I T C A P A C I T Y D P B D Q L P I
E U T I S O P E D F O E T A C I F I T R E C I D
H N T F G Z Y B D U G Q A R M P V N G C B Z E E
C D Z S C R C R K E C T E X I X U S T D A Z C R
D F D R E R O H O M D D E L E O W R B L N V E C
E I P E P R W S Z T I U S G C Q O K C C K J W D
C N E Y K D E K S T S T C C D N G A B D S X O E
N A H X Z J C T O E I I A T I U N B L F T S R D
U N L I S E V R N S A S H C I C B I E W A N K N
O C X U H G S A O I G R F T E O A Z O U T W G E
B I G C K D D P V N D U N L I C N Y M X E Y L N
B A C V O O E L I M N N E I U D Q S A O M O K E
P L J Q Y D Z V N D T D U H N B E X Q P E R D P
F M I D W B A F S O C P A O X G A R W I N S D O
I A G P F S P T C H L Q M E P E S X C O T E R R
R N U P O H R H E D U G R N H M E D Z V X X A C
J A A W F A J C I H F Q U K R D O S I Z J A D C
U G P K N R K C R E T S I G E R K C E H C T S D
J E X S E N D O R S E M E N T F G F Q H P C S G
H M F N G L T F Z Y Z M U A Q E Y I Z R X T O K
Q E T S E R E T N I L M C K T S X R A U I T A P
R N Q Q A S J Q Y O D N X G W M U G X F I V U Y
G T E Z D Q D X G V D K R G G E Z O T S P G M J
```

Checking Your Location

For each of the following statements, write **F** if the statement is more false than true. Write **T** if the statement is more true than false.

_____ **1.** Financial goals are influenced by personal interests and values, and these goals never change.

_____ **2.** Your employer is legally responsible for withholding local, state, and federal taxes from your earnings.

_____ **3.** Income tax returns must be filed by April 15 for the preceding calendar year.

_____ **4.** A checking account is a useful financial-management tool.

_____ **5.** The amount of interest that a savings account earns depends on the amount of money deposited and the rate of interest being paid, but not on how often the interest is paid.

_____ **6.** A savings account can be opened in a number of financial institutions—including banks, savings and loan associations, credit unions, brokerages, and other financial services companies—and with the federal government.

_____ **7.** A good credit rating is one of the most valuable financial tools you have.

_____ **8.** Credit worthiness revolves around the three C's of credit: character, capacity, and capital.

_____ **9.** People with previous credit problems rarely pay a higher interest rate than people with good credit.

_____ **10.** A bank's lending requirements are usually the same as those of other types of lending institutions.

_____ **11.** Banks join the MasterCard or Visa multipurpose credit card system to earn money.

_____ **12.** Federal law sets interest rates and other credit charges.

_____ **13.** A finance charge is the interest charge paid to use credit.

On a separate sheet of paper, rewrite the statements you marked false and make them true. Include the number of each statement you write.

Being a Wise Consumer

Chapter **18**

How Do You Manage Money?

Financial management is a key to reaching your life goals. It is also a method of meeting future financial crises. In this activity, you will evaluate how you spend your money.

In the first column, list 10 goods or services that you have frequently purchased with your money. In the second column, rank the ways you spent money in the order of their importance to you. Let 1 be the most important and 10 be the least important. Review the decision-making styles described in Chapter 4 (authority, fatalistic, intuitive, impulsive, rational). In the last column, write the style of decision making you used for each purchase listed in the first column.

Ways I Spent Money	Importance Ranking	Decision-Making Style Used

Total the number of spending decisions you made using each decision-making style:

Authority: ___   Fatalistic: ___   Intuitive: ___   Impulsive: ___   Rational: ___

1. Which of your decisions and decision-making styles are you most satisfied with? Why?

_____

_____

2. Which of your decisions and decision-making styles are you least satisfied with? Why?

_____

_____

Necessities and Frills

An important part of a successful budget is being a prudent consumer—getting the most for your money, recognizing quality, avoiding waste, and realizing time cost as well as money cost in making consumer decisions.

Refer to the "Develop a Successful Budget" activity in Chapter 17 of this activity book. In that activity, you assumed that you were living on your own and had a job that paid $3,200 a month ($38,400 a year). These earnings would equal $738.46 a week.

1. How much did you allow for food at home and away from home per month? _____

   Per year? _____

2. What would be your average weekly food costs? (Divide your yearly food budget by 52.) _____

In Figure 18.1 in the textbook, you learned that the average amount allotted to food purchases, both at home and away from home, equals 9.8 percent of spending per year. Using the income from the "Develop a Successful Budget" activity in Chapter 17, figure out the average amount allotted to total food expenses for the following:

1. The average yearly amount allotted to total food expenses for yearly earnings of $38,400.

   _____

2. The average monthly amount allotted to food expenses for monthly earnings of $3,200.

   _____

3. The average weekly amount allotted to food expenses for weekly earnings of $738.46.

   _____

4. Was the amount of money you allotted in your budget for food more, less, or nearly the same as this?

   _____

5. The average amount spent on food at home is 5.8 percent. What is 5.8 percent of $738.46?

   _____

6. The average amount spent on food away from home is 4 percent. What is 4 percent of $738.46?

   _____

Assume that you are living on your own and have $64.98 to spend on food you will eat at home and $47.26 to spend on food you will eat away from home in a week. Use the format that follows and write a menu for each meal you will eat during the week. Mark the meals you plant to eat at home with an **H**. Mark those you plan to eat away from home with an **R**.

Weekly Menu Plan

	Breakfast	Lunch	Dinner	Snacks
Monday				
Tuesday				
Wednesday				
Thursday				
Friday				
Saturday				
Sunday				

Use the following chart to make a shopping list for the groceries you would need to purchase with your weekly eat-at-home budget of $64.98. Go to a grocery store to research prices of each food item you need.

Try to find the lowest price for each item. Before you shop, clip food coupons from the Sunday newspaper. Also, read the food ads in the newspaper before deciding which store to go to because you can save money on sale items. Also note that some stores offer double coupons. In these stores, the coupons are worth twice their printed value. Compare the prices of different brands, including house brands, to see how much you can save by purchasing one brand rather than another. When possible, use unit pricing information (the price per measure or unit in weight, volume, count, or area) to make comparisons. Unit pricing information is usually located on the shelf edge, directly below the item.

A Weekly Grocery List

Food Item	Name of Brand	Coupon Savings	Unit Price	Total Price
Final total:				

1. Where did you shop? _____

2. Were you able to stay within the $64.98 budget for food you will eat at home? _____

   If you went over the $64.98 budget, redo your weekly menu and grocery list and shop again for the items you need.

3. Would you be able to plan a menu and meet this food budget for a family of four? Explain your answer.

   _____

   _____

4. What are three food shopping tips you learned from this experience?

   _____

   _____

   _____

List the meals in your menu that you plan to eat away from home. Check restaurant prices for those meals and fill in the following chart.

1. What was your total for restaurant meals? _____

2. Were you able to stay within the $47.26 budget for food eaten away from home? _____

3. Some people use part of their entertainment budget for eating in restaurants. Would you use some of the money from your entertainment budget for eating away from home? _____
   If so, how much?_____

Weekly Restaurant Budget

	Breakfast	Lunch	Dinner	Snacks
Monday				
Tuesday				
Wednesday				
Thursday				
Friday				
Saturday				
Sunday				
Total:				

Advertisements in the Media

Advertising is communicated to us through newspapers, magazines, billboards, radio, television, junk mail, and motion pictures. Each year, businesses spend large sums of money to determine what will cause consumers to buy a particular product. Advertisements teach us what to want. They are a powerful influence on our attitudes toward a product or service.

Cut out at least 15 newspaper and magazine ads that appeal to you. The ads should describe products that you want to purchase now or in the future. Use the ads to answer the following questions. In your answers, list the product names that apply and explain how each of those ads makes its appeal.

1. Which ads appeal to your self-esteem and your desire for social approval?

   _____

   _____

   _____

2. Which ads appeal to your desire for romance and affection?

   _____

   _____

   _____

3. Which ads appeal to your desire for good health and long life?

   _____

   _____

   _____

4. Which ads appeal to your desire to make a lot of money and be wealthy?

   _____

   _____

   _____

5. Which ads appeal to your intellect?

   _____

   _____

   _____

6. Which ads appeal to your desire to be happy and enjoy life?

   _____

   _____

   _____

List *all* the brand names of clothes and shoes in your closet.

_____

_____

_____

_____

_____

_____

1. What advertisements influenced you to buy those particular brands?

_____

_____

_____

_____

2. Which brand names lived up to their advertising claims?

_____

_____

_____

_____

3. What is most influential in making you choose one product over another? Why?

_____

_____

_____

_____

_____

Finding a Place to Live

Housing costs will probably make up the largest part of your budget.

1. Refer again to the "Develop a Successful Budget" activity in Chapter 17 of this activity book. How much did you allow for rent or mortgage payment per month?

   _____

   Per year? _____

2. In Figure 18.1 in your textbook, you learned that the average amount allotted to housing averages 24 percent of spending. (This amount includes utilities, insurance, furnishings, and maintenance costs.) Using the income from the budget activity in Chapter 17, figure out the average amount allotted to total housing expenses for average monthly earnings of $3,200.

   _____

3. Was the amount of money you allotted in your budget for housing (including utilities, insurance, furnishings, and maintenance costs) more, less, or nearly the same as this?

   _____

4. In this activity, assume that you are getting ready to rent an apartment on your own and have $1001.60 to spend on housing. How much of your housing budget will you allow for utilities, insurance, furnishings, and maintenance costs?

   _____

5. How much does that leave for the rent on the apartment? (If you will have a roommate, you can share the rental expenses and might possibly afford a more expensive apartment.)

   _____

Check the classified advertisements in your newspaper for apartments or houses for rent. Look until you find a rental that fits your budget. Arrange to visit an apartment you are interested in and evaluate its features. Fill in the following information and then use the following survey to evaluate the apartment.

Apartment #: _____

Address: _____

Date viewed: _____

Rent: _____

Approximate utility costs: _____

Deposit: _____

Length of lease:_____

Date available: _____

Rental agent's fee: _____

Rental agent or owner name: _____

Phone number: _____

Number of bedrooms: _____

Number of baths: _____

Type of heat/air: _____

Rate each of the items listed below according to the following scale.

Rating Scale: 1 = Not acceptable; 2 = Below average; 3 = Average; 4 = Above average;
5 = Very exceptional.

____	Number of rooms	____	Trash/garbage collection
____	Condition of interior walls	____	Soundproof to outside noises
____	Closet/storage space	____	Neighborhood
____	Cable TV	____	Condition of grounds
____	Screens, storm windows	____	Recreation facilities
____	Air conditioning	____	Security at night
____	Carpeting, blinds, drapes	____	Parking facilities
____	Laundry facilities	____	Neighborhood traffic
____	Soundproof to noises in other apartments		Convenience to
____	Appliances	____	Work
____	Smoke detector/fire alarm	____	Public transportation
____	Fire escape/fire exit	____	Supermarket
____	Door and window locks	____	Shopping
____	Security system	____	Child care
____	Furniture (if furnished)	____	Hospitals
____	Kitchen and bathroom	____	Recreation/parks
____	Odors from other apartments	____	Restaurants/entertainment
____	Restrictions on children/pets	____	Place of worship
____	Age mix of renters	____	School/college
____	Repairs and maintenance	____	Rent
____	Mailbox	____	Utilities

You have rated 41 important areas related to the apartment. Total all 41 ratings:_____

A perfect rating is 205; the average is 123. If your overall satisfaction with the apartment is less than 123, you will probably be dissatisfied with the apartment.

Before you sign a lease to rent an apartment, it is a good idea to evaluate it in terms of your personal lifestyle. Review your 41 total ratings. Circle the 10 ratings that are most important to you in terms of your personal values and lifestyle.

Total your 10 most important ratings: _____

A perfect rating is 50; the average is 30. If the 10 ratings that are most important to you total less than 30, continue searching for a suitable apartment. If they total 30 or more, use the rational approach to decision making before signing a lease.

Purchasing Your First Automobile

Buying a new car is usually the second most expensive purchase consumers make. Refer to the "Develop a Successful Budget" activity in Chapter 17 of this activity book. Total the amounts you budgeted for monthly transportation expenses, including the loan payment on a vehicle, fuel, repairs, auto insurance, parking, and public transportation.

1. How much did you allow for transportation expenses per month? _____

2. In Figure 18.1 in your textbook, you learned that the average amount allotted to transportation, not including auto insurance, equals 15.2 percent of spending. (This amount includes private vehicles, gasoline and motor oil, and other forms of transportation.) Using the income from the budget you created in Chapter 17, figure out the average amount allotted to total transportation expenses for average monthly earnings of $3,200.

_____

3. Was this amount of money more, less, or nearly the same as the amount that you budgeted for?

_____

Most new car dealers will negotiate on price and bargain on their profit margin, which is generally between 15 and 20 percent. This is usually the difference between the manufacturer's suggested retail price and the invoice price. (You can find the invoice price by looking at the dealer's invoice or by reviewing new car publications.)

Key to Success: When buying a new or used car, remember that you are in charge of the sale, not the dealer. Don't be afraid to walk away. If you shop at several dealerships, you might save a small percentage, but that small percentage could amount to a lot of money on this big-ticket item.

Visit a new car dealer and use the following worksheet to compare the invoice price and the retail price of a new car of your choice. Reread the section "Buying a New Car" in Chapter 18 before you visit the dealer to make certain that you understand how automobiles are priced.

Name of dealer you visited: _____

Car make and model: _____

Worksheet for Buying a New Car

Options	Invoice Price	Retail Price

Transmission:
    Automatic
    Stick		

Sound System:
    AM-FM radio
    CD player		

Power brakes		
Rear window defogger		

Tires:
    Full-size spare
    Steel-belted radials		

Other		

Other		
Other		
Air conditioning		

Engine:
    Size
    Diesel		

Power steering		
Power locks		
Power seats		
Rear window wiper/washer		
Luggage rack		

Mirrors:
    Dual
    Dual remote
    Passenger visor		

Other		
Other		

Consumers frequently purchase expensive but unimportant options. Review the options listed on your worksheet. Circle the four that are most important to you. Draw a line through the four that are least important to you.

Show the dealer the options you consider important and those you consider unimportant. New car options are usually sold in groups. Ask your dealer to show you prices on option groups as well as individual option prices. Can you save money this way?

As a first-time car buyer, you are beginning your "rite of passage" from childhood to being a full-fledged American adult. You have examined the sticker price and invoice cost with and without certain options, kicked the tires, and opened and closed all of the doors at least 20 times (including a minimum of 4 slams). You have placed your head under the hood with your nose no more than 4 inches from the strange-looking metal things and have impressed the dealer with your knowledgeable grunts and humming noises. Now it is time to negotiate a price.

1. Total the dealer's invoice cost and the options you want. _____

2. Calculate 15 percent of the total. (The dealer expects to make a profit of 15 to 20 percent.)

_____

3. Total the invoice cost plus 15 percent. _____

This is your offer.

Finding the Right Words

Chapter 18 of your textbook contains numerous terms that employers and workers use. Recognizing and understanding these terms will help you make the important career decisions you will soon face. Unscramble the terms in column B, and match them with the definitions in column A. (Some terms may contain two words.)

Column A	Column B
Example: _a_ unsolicited commercial e-mail	a. _____spam_____ apms
1. ___ buying products to impress others	b. _____ cineerg
2. ___ promoting the sale of a product or service or advancing an idea	c. _____ rytwanar
3. ___ having no trademark	d. _____ cunaserni
4. ___ the cost of one standard measure of a product	e. _____ uremmip
5. ___ a contract that involves a financial commitment	f. _____ cienivo cirep
6. ___ unsteady, irregular	g. _____ blayiliti eroveagc
7. ___ a person who rents another person's building or land	h. _____ tenpdur
8. ___ wise, shrewd, and frugal	i. _____ ryitecus tespoid
9. ___ a guarantee that a product is of a certain quality or that defective parts will be replaced	j. _____ selea
10. ___ insurance for bodily injuries, property damages, and medical expenses when you are at fault	k. _____ tranoloopim lasse
11. ___ the automobile manufacturer's initial charge to the dealer	l. _____ itun cirep
12. ___ guaranteeing property or a person against loss or harm	m. _____ natten
13. ___ money you entrust with the landlord to cover any damage you cause to the rental unit	n. _____ lutgucifant
14. ___ the policyholder's payment for an insurance policy	o. _____ rivatingeds
15. ___ temporary price reductions on regular merchandise	p. _____ occosupunis pontusicomn

Checking Your Location

For each of the following statements, write **F** if the statement is more false than true. Write **T** if the statement is more true than false.

____ **1.** You share responsibility for final decisions about your consumer purchases with your friends and family.

____ **2.** Merchants do not have to give you a rain check for an advertised product.

____ **3.** The unit price can help you compare the price of products that have different weights or volumes.

____ **4.** The type of store where you shop has little to do with the prices you pay.

____ **5.** Conspicuous consumption can be very costly if you are living on a tight budget.

____ **6.** Promotional sales promote regular merchandise through temporary price reductions.

____ **7.** Advertising is intended to promote the sale of a product or service, to advance an idea, or to bring about some other effect that the advertiser desires.

____ **8.** You should beware of products or services if the manufacturer or service provider will not back its claims with a written guarantee.

____ **9.** Food costs will probably make up the largest part of your living expenses.

____ **10.** A general rule is to allow no more than one-half of your take-home pay for housing.

____ **11.** It is wise to talk with other residents in a rental complex about their likes and dislikes before you sign a lease to live at that complex.

____ **12.** Before moving into an apartment, it is a good consumer practice to make an inventory of all items furnished in the rental unit, to rate the condition of the furnishings and the overall condition of the unit, and to have the inventory signed and dated by you and the landlord.

____ **13.** The responsibilities of both the tenant and the landlord are defined in a lease; both parties are legally required to live up to the signed agreement.

On a separate sheet of paper, rewrite the statements you marked false and make them true. Include the number of each statement you write.

Achieving Wellness

Chapter **19**

Nutrition Facts

Learn to read the facts on the nutrition labels before you decide which products to purchase. This information can help you select a healthy diet.

For this activity, select two different brands of cereal to compare and evaluate for nutritive value. Using the following chart, compare and evaluate the nutritional information on the labels of the two cereals.

	Cereal 1	Cereal 2
Product name		
Serving size		
Calories in a serving		
Total fat		
Saturated fat		
Cholesterol		
Sodium		
Total carbohydrates		
Dietary fiber		
Sugar		
Protein		

1. Which two vitamins and minerals in Cereal 1 have the highest percentage of daily value?

   _____

2. Which two vitamins and minerals in Cereal 2 have the highest percentage of daily value?

   _____

3. Name two vitamins and minerals you need each day that are not listed on the cereal boxes.

   _____

4. The American Heart Association recommends that your total fat intake be less than 30 percent of your total calories. So if you consume 2,500 calories per day, you should eat fewer than 80 grams of fat per day. If you consume 2,000 calories or less per day, you should eat fewer than 65 grams of fat per day. Which cereal would be most healthful in terms of fat content? _____

5. Taking all the nutritional information into account, which cereal do you think would be the healthiest choice? Why?

   _____

   _____

You Are What You Eat

Government nutrition guidelines recommend that you eat 6 to 11 servings of bread, cereal, and pasta (preferably whole grain); 3 to 5 servings of vegetables; 2 to 4 servings of fruit; 2 or 3 servings of dairy products; and 2 or 3 servings of meat, beans, eggs or nuts every day. If that sounds like a lot of food, keep in mind that a serving of bread is one slice, and one large banana is two servings of fruit. You also should use oils and sweets sparingly.

Select one day from the Weekly Menu Plan you created in the "Necessities and Frills" worksheet in Chapter 18, and record how many servings of each of the food groups you had in your menu that day. Use the nutrition labels to help you figure out serving sizes.

1. Which day did you pick? _____

2. What did you eat from the bread, cereal, and pasta group? List the number of servings and type of food.

   _____

   _____

3. What did you eat from the vegetable group? List the number of servings and type of food.

   _____

   _____

4. What did you eat from the fruit group? List the number of servings and type of food.

   _____

   _____

5. What did you eat from the dairy group? List the number of servings and type of food.

   _____

   _____

6. What did you eat from the meat, beans, and nuts group? List the number of servings and type of food.

   _____

   _____

7. Did your menu have the recommended number of servings of the five major food groups? _____

8. In which food groups were you lacking?

   _____

   _____

9. In which food groups were you about right?

   _____

   _____

10. What changes do you need to make for a healthier diet?

   _____

   _____

Rewrite your menu to reflect these changes. Mark those that you plan to eat away from home with a **R.** Mark the meals you plan to eat at home with a **H.**

Weekly Menu Plan

	Breakfast	**Lunch**	**Dinner**	**Snacks**
Monday				
Tuesday				
Wednesday				
Thursday				
Friday				
Saturday				
Sunday				

Name _____ **Class** _____ **Date** _____

Too Much Stress

We experience stress all the time, but too much stress can seriously affect our physical and mental well-being. Consider the situation of Marcee Jahonovich.

Marcee is 16 years old and in the 11th grade of Harborview High School. Marcee's parents divorced four years ago. She lives with her mother during the school year and spends vacations and summers with her father. Her mother plans to remarry next summer. Her father remarried three years ago and has two stepchildren from his second marriage. Marcee has gone steady with Perry for more than a year. Perry and her best friend, Janet, have helped her deal with the stress in her family life.

Last month, Perry broke up with Marcee. She has been very depressed, and last week she told Janet that she has even considered suicide. Janet spent the night with Marcee and convinced her to get professional help. The next morning, Marcee and Janet visited their school counselor. The counselor convinced Marcee to visit a clinical psychologist.

Marcee is lucky. She had a good friend to help her with a personal crisis. The school counselor brought Marcee and her mother together to face the situation, and the psychologist is helping all of them deal with the problems that caused Marcee's depression.

At first, Marcee blamed her depression on Perry for breaking off their relationship. Now she understands that a lot of factors were involved in her depression. She is rapidly learning life skills that are helping her improve her mental health.

Marcee has learned to get her daily tasks done without making other people angry. This life skill has helped her improve her relationship with her mother and some of her teachers. She has learned to recognize her personal feelings and to express them in a way that is acceptable to others. Getting her feelings out in the open has relieved a lot of Marcee's depression and anger.

When Marcee is unhappy, she has learned to do something positive to solve her problem rather than going to her room and brooding about it. Sometimes, a simple change of pace takes her out of the unhappy mood.

Marcee isn't trying to regain her mental health overnight. Instead, she is moving ahead one step at a time. She has discovered that the slow process of working toward solutions gives her a strong feeling of hope for her future. Even on a bad day, she no longer feels trapped.

1. We all need to love and be loved. What situations in Marcee's life might have caused her to feel unloved?

   _____

   _____

2. What situations might have caused Marcee to feel loved?

   _____

   _____

3. We all need to belong and to be accepted by others. What situations in Marcee's life might have caused her to feel alone or rejected?

   _____

   _____

4. What situations might have caused her to feel as if she belonged and was accepted?

_____

_____

5. We all need to feel we are worthwhile. What situations in Marcee's life might have caused her to feel hopeless and sad?

_____

_____

6. What situations in Marcee's life caused her to feel she was important to someone?

_____

_____

7. For what emotional needs did Marcee rely on Janet? _____

_____

8. For what emotional needs did Marcee rely on Perry? _____

_____

9. Who makes you feel worthwhile and special? _____

10. Who feels worthwhile and special because of you? _____

11. Who makes you feel lovable? _____

12. Who feels lovable because of you? _____

13. Who accepts you for who you are? _____

14. Who feels accepted because of you? _____

Marcee has discovered that she has feelings of love, self-worth, being accepted, and being special, and that they are important to her. She has also discovered that other people have the same feelings. Marcee understands that having her feelings ignored made her feel angry and depressed. Now, when her feelings are hurt by the important people in her life, she still feels sad, but instead of being angry or depressed, Marcee tries to say or do something to let the other person know that she understands their anger and loves them. The more she helps and understands others, the easier it is to ignore her feelings of anger and depression.

Briefly describe a recent situation in which you felt angry or depressed because your feelings were hurt.

_____

_____

_____

_____

Did you like your reaction? If so, why? If not, describe a better reaction for a similar situation.

_____

_____

_____

_____

Read the Instructions Carefully

The label on a bottle of prescription medicine is an important source of information for the patient. Read the information on a bottle of prescription medicine, and answer the following questions.

1. What dosage is prescribed (liquid, capsules, tablets)? _____

2. What is the strength of the medicine (usually given in milligrams or mgs)?_____

3. What is the total amount the patient will receive (15 capsules, 5 fluid ounces)?_____

4. What are the directions for use? (These are often abbreviations of Latin words. For instance, *terin die,* written *t.i.d.,* means three times per day.)

_____

5. How many times can the prescription be refilled?_____

Surveys show that in 9 out of 10 cases, we take care of our everyday aches and pains without going to a health professional. We tough it out, use a home remedy, or buy an over-the-counter (OTC) product. These medications range from allergy medicine to antacids, painkillers, and laxatives. The Federal Drug Administration requires that OTC labels be much more detailed than prescription drug labels so that consumers can properly use the products without the advice of a health professional. It is the consumer's responsibility to read the label and follow the instructions.

Read the information on a bottle of OTC medication, and answer the following questions.

1. What is the name of the OTC medication?_____

2. What are the suggested uses? _____

_____

3. Is the product sealed for your protection? _____

4. What are the active ingredients? _____

_____

5. What are the inactive ingredients? _____

_____

6. What is the net quantity of the contents? _____

7. What are the name and address of the manufacturer, packer, or distributor?

_____

_____

8. What are the directions and dosage instructions? (Summarize these.)

_____

_____

9. What are the warnings, cautionary statements, and drug-interaction precautions (if any)?

_____

_____

10. What is the expiration date of the medication? _____

Safety in the Workplace

Many of the factors involved in personal health and safety on the job can be controlled. Read the following two case studies regarding workplace safety and answer the questions.

It was Tyrone's first day on the job with the E.W. Heslop Chair Company. The supervisor asked Tyrone if he knew how to operate a table saw. Tyrone explained that he had never used that type of tool. The supervisor demonstrated how to use a pattern and cut pieces of wood for a chair frame. Within 20 minutes, the supervisor returned to her office, and Tyrone was working alone. An hour later, Tyrone's scream pierced the air, louder than all the noisy machines in the shop. Tyrone made one mistake: He forgot to use one safety device and lost his right hand forever.

1. What action could the supervisor have taken to prevent this accident?

_____

2. What action could Tyrone have taken to prevent this accident?

_____

3. Who is responsible for this accident? Explain your point of view.

_____

_____

_____

_____

Margo is a machinist employed by the West Shore Tool and Die Corporation. Frank operates an overhead crane. He moves large metal dies and lowers them to Margo's machine. When Margo is finished with a die, Frank uses the crane to remove it. Margo remains in the area under the crane to give Frank hand signals. Frank provides similar assistance to several machinists.

Last week, Margo discovered that Frank has a drinking problem. While helping him lift a 50-pound tool by hand, Margo noticed the odor of alcohol on Frank's breath. During a break, she noticed the odor of alcohol coming from Frank's thermos bottle. Margo also noticed that Frank occasionally slurs his speech. Four days later, Frank's crane dropped a metal die on one of Margo's coworkers. The plant security officer proved that Frank was intoxicated at the time of the accident. The coworker remains in critical condition.

1. What action could Frank have taken to prevent this accident?

_____

2. What action could Margo have taken to prevent this accident?

_____

3. Who is responsible for this accident? Explain your point of view.

_____

_____

_____

_____

The Surgeon General Warns

The following information about the negative effect of tobacco products and alcoholic beverages is common knowledge to most teenagers and adults. Review the information; then complete the activity that follows.

The smoking of tobacco products is the chief avoidable cause of death in our society. Smokers are more likely than nonsmokers to contract heart disease. Indeed, some 170,000 die each year from smoking-related coronary heart disease. Lung, larynx, esophageal, bladder, pancreatic, and kidney cancers also strike smokers at increased rates.

This information is taught to students from the time they are in the intermediate grades of elementary school, yet too many young people ignore the dangers and start to smoke. The following reasons are frequently given for why young people smoke: peer pressure, increased popularity, family problems, home smoking habits, "for kicks," to appear grown up, and lack of knowledge of the effects of smoking on the human body.

Imagine that you work on the Surgeon General's staff and are assigned to develop a campaign to keep teenagers from smoking. What would you do? Use the information in this activity to develop a successful campaign.

_____

_____

_____

_____

_____

_____

_____

_____

_____

_____

_____

_____

_____

_____

_____

_____

_____

_____

_____

_____

Name_____ Class_____ Date_____

Finding the Right Words

Chapter 19 of your textbook contains numerous terms that employers and workers use. Recognizing and understanding these terms will help you make the important career decisions you will soon face. Write a short story using the following vocabulary terms. Make certain that you understand the definition of each term before you use it in your story.

aerobic	drug abuse	muscular strength
calorie	flexibility	nutrients
cardiorespiratory endurance	hospitalization insurance	Occupational Safety and Health Administration (OSHA)
diet	mandated	Recommended Daily Allowances (RDAs)
drug	muscular endurance	stress
		surgical insurance

Title: _____

_____
_____
_____
_____
_____
_____
_____
_____
_____
_____
_____
_____
_____
_____
_____
_____
_____
_____
_____
_____
_____
_____

Checking Your Location

For each of the following statements, write **F** if the statement is more false than true. Write **T** if the statement is more true than false.

____ **1.** The quality of all aspects of your life is affected by your physical and mental condition.

____ **2.** If you eat more food than your body requires, the extra food can be changed into fat tissue, which does not promote good health.

____ **3.** RDAs are the same for everybody, regardless of your age, gender, or weight.

____ **4.** Fat contains fewer calories than an equal amount of carbohydrates or protein.

____ **5.** To get all the vitamins, minerals, and fiber your body needs, you should eat a lot of meat and cheese.

____ **6.** Exercise increases your body's ability to transport oxygen to your cells, and oxygen is a key ingredient in physical activities.

____ **7.** It typically takes a week or two of regular exercise to realize the benefits of a fitness program.

____ **8.** The chief villain of skin cancer are the sun's ultraviolet rays.

____ **9.** Drugs are the number-one killer of children in America.

____ **10.** You probably have good mental health if you truthfully consider yourself to be competent, loved, and liked.

____ **11.** Pharmacists dispense more than two billion prescriptions a year, but up to half of the people do not use them as prescribed.

____ **12.** Doing the same motions over and over again at work is sometimes boring, but it's never harmful.

____ **13.** Many companies require employees to accept random drug and alcohol testing as a condition of employment.

____ **14.** When people exhibit sudden negative changes in their behavior, it should be a matter of concern.

____ **15.** Self-confidence and a positive attitude toward other people and life situations play an important role in avoiding the temptation to abuse drugs.

On a separate sheet of paper, rewrite the statements you marked false and make them true. Include the number of each statement you write.

Accepting Civic Responsibility

Chapter **20**

Being a Responsible Citizen

"And for the support of this Declaration, with a firm reliance on the protection of divine providence, we mutually pledge to each other our lives, our fortunes, and our sacred honor." As the closing statement to the Declaration of Independence, this pledge of civic responsibility is as true today as it was when it was written.

Whether at home or overseas, thousands of Americans have pledged their lives to help during local and national emergencies caused by criminal activities, fires, wars, floods, famines, storms, and earthquakes. List six occupations that require workers to pledge their lives and write down the services these workers provide.

Occupational Title	Service Provided

In the modern world, fortunes in the form of taxes must be pledged by responsible citizens to provide many of the services they have come to expect. Review your list of workers and the services they provide. Draw a line through the occupations and services that are funded with tax revenue.

Review the tax-funded occupations and services you have identified. Describe how these occupations will affect your future.

Occupation: _____

Expected effect on my lifestyle and career:

_____

_____

_____

Occupation: _____

Expected effect on my lifestyle and career:

_____

_____

_____

Occupation: _____

Expected effect on my lifestyle and career:

_____

_____

_____

Imagine that it is 20 years from now, and you have achieved your major personal and career goals. Write a paragraph explaining some ways you will demonstrate your civic responsibility.

_____

_____

_____

_____

_____

_____

_____

_____

_____

_____

_____

_____

_____

_____

_____

_____

_____

_____

_____

_____

_____

_____

_____

_____

What's Your Opinion?

Most citizens agree on what the major social problems are, but they frequently disagree on the "right" way to solve them. In this activity, you will poll at least five people regarding the following social problem and ask them the question that follows. Use the space provided to record the information from your poll.

The issue: Crimes of violence and America's youth

Have the people you survey read these facts before responding:

- Homicides of youth from the ages of 5 through 19 on school property, on the way to or from school, and while attending or traveling from a school-sponsored event totaled 24 for the years 2000 through 2002.

- Homicides away from school totaled 2,045 for the 2000–2001 school year.

- Juvenile arrests for murder, forcible rape, robbery, and aggravated assault in 2002 totaled 71,059.

- The percentage of students in grades 9 through 12 who reported carrying a weapon on school property in 2001 (at least one day) during the previous 30 days totaled 6.4 percent.

- The percentage of students in grades 9 through 12 who reported carrying a weapon anywhere in 2001 (at least one day) during the previous 30 days totaled 17.4 percent.

- The Second Amendment to the U.S. Constitution reads as follows: "A well regulated Militia, being necessary to the security of a free State, the right of the people to keep and bear Arms, shall not be infringed."

The question: Would harsher punishment for violent offenders slow down violent crime involving youth in America? Why or why not? What is the solution to the problem?

Respondent 1

Name_____ Age_____ Sex _____

Answer _____

Reason _____

Solution _____

Respondent 2

Name_____ Age_____ Sex _____

Answer _____

Reason _____

Solution _____

Respondent 3

Name_____ Age_____ Sex _____

Answer _____

Reason _____

Solution _____

Respondent 4

Name_____ Age_____ Sex _____

Answer _____

Reason _____

Solution _____

Respondent 5

Name_____ Age_____ Sex _____

Answer _____

Reason _____

Solution _____

1. Assume that your poll is representative of all of the citizens in the United States. What would your survey report as the perceived solution to the problem?

   _____

   _____

2. Which of your respondents had the most facts or evidence to support his or her opinion?

   _____

3. Who had the strongest feelings about this problem?_____

4. Had any of your respondents ever been the victim of a violent crime? If so, how did this influence his or her opinion?

   _____

   _____

5. In your opinion, what is the cause of the increase in violent crime in the United States?

   _____

   _____

6. What do you believe is the solution to this problem?

   _____

   _____

7. What are the benefits of your solution for you and your friends?

   _____

   _____

8. What consequences must we face if we do not resolve this problem?

   _____

   _____

Finding the Right Words

Chapter 20 of your textbook contains numerous terms that employers and workers use. Recognizing and understanding these terms will help you make the important career decisions you will soon face.

Unscramble the terms in Column **B** and match them with the definitions in column **A.** (Some terms contain two or more words.)

Column A	Column B
Example: _a_ vital statistics of the human population	a. _____demographics_____ hemapogicrsd
1. ____ citizens' duties to the laws and policies of their community, state, and nation	b. _____ ciicv yesnolipsitbir
2. ____ indifference	c. _____ hamisarc
3. ____ newspapers, magazines, radio, and television	d. _____ haytap
4. ____ an appealing leadership quality	e. _____ adime
5. ____ the highest law in the country	f. _____ tyroppre axt
6. ____ a tax that depends on property ownership	g. _____ ureeven
7. ____ seeing one side of an issue as totally right or wrong	h. _____ S.U. nonoititstuC
8. ____ income	i. _____ noiiratazlop fo sueiss
9. ____ laws, edicts, or decrees enacted by a local government	j. _____ cansordine
10. ____ the population of an area divided by its square miles	k. _____ moecin axt
11. ____ a body of rules that a nation, state, or community recognizes as binding on its citizens	l. _____ swal
12. ____ a tax based on a citizen's earnings	m. _____ trainmeetld
13. ____ lacking individuality	n. _____ cialos yynotimna
14. ____ damaging	o. _____ planoipout ytnedis

Checking Your Location

For each of the following statements, write **F** if the statement is more false than true. Write **T** if the statement is more true than false.

____ **1.** The United States has the most restrictions on voting of any country in the world.

____ **2.** The U.S. government is the largest employer and purchaser of goods and services in our economy.

____ **3.** Most registered voters inform themselves equally about all sides of an issue or about all political viewpoints on an issue.

____ **4.** Public services are paid for through taxes.

____ **5.** Most of the taxes you will pay during your working years will go to the state government.

____ **6.** The federal government makes decisions with which each citizen must live.

____ **7.** The United States' relationship with other countries doesn't affect your daily life.

____ **8.** Each citizen's rights and privileges end where his or her neighbor's rights and privileges begin.

____ **9.** Most citizens agree that the resolution of social problems is beyond the control of one person or group and requires collective action from all citizens.

____ **10.** Between 1960 and 2000, the proportion of immigrants from Europe increased from 74.5 percent to 87.1 percent.

____ **11.** Advances in modern industry, technology, and agriculture have improved our standard of living and the environment.

____ **12.** The Department of Homeland Security is responsible for protecting air travel, ports, and waterways.

____ **13.** As the level of educational achievement goes higher, the difference between the income of men and women or between races decreases.

____ **14.** Growth rates of 1.9 percent and higher will double a population in about 36 years.

On a separate sheet of paper, rewrite the statements you marked false and make them true. Include the number of each statement you write.

Balancing Your Career and Your Life

Going Through the Stages

Every basic life skill you learn paves the way for further learning. You probably learned the life skills listed as follows before you were seven years old. In each case, what further learning did you accomplish? Describe two specific job skills that are directly related to this life skill.

Example: Learning to walk led to <u>running, skipping, riding a bicycle, skating, hiking, and athletic skills.</u>

Two related job skills are <u>a construction worker climbing on a scaffold and a firefighter moving quickly to rescue people in a fire.</u>

Learning to talk led to _____

Two related job skills are _____

_____

Learning to trust others led to _____

Two related job skills are _____

_____

Learning to manipulate objects led to _____

Two related job skills are _____

_____

Learning to be independent led to _____

Two related job skills are _____

_____

Learning how to read and write led to _____

Two related job skills are _____

_____

The Working Years

People frequently refer to the broad range of time between the late twenties and the middle sixties as *the working years*. Before you answer the following questions, think of the personal and career roles you want to have during your working years.

1. What career role would you like? _____

2. Would this career role make you feel like a productive member of society? Why or why not?

_____

_____

3. What family roles would you like (parent, son, daughter, aunt, uncle)?

_____

4. Which of these family roles would be most important to you? Why?

_____

_____

5. What will you do to help prepare the next generation for family responsibilities and future careers?

_____

_____

_____

6. Will you help society to protect the knowledge and products of past generations? If so, how? If not, why not?

_____

_____

_____

List three actions you are presently involved in or have completed to prepare yourself for the working years.

_____

_____

_____

List three actions you are planning to begin during the next two years to prepare yourself for the working years.

_____

_____

_____

_____

Name_____ Class_____ Date_____

Rate Your Date

Dating provides two people with an opportunity to discover and understand each other's interests, values, and attitudes. If they identify several similarities, they may want to continue dating and eventually enter a period of courtship.

Use the following scale to rate each of the 10 dating activities listed in the following chart. Ask the person you are dating or a good friend to rate the 10 activities. Read the statements to your date or friend and record his or her answers. Don't reveal your answers until your date or friend has completed his or her responses. Read the results together.

Rating Scale: 1 = I would enjoy this activity very much. 2 = I would enjoy this activity. 3 = I have no strong feelings about this activity. 4 = I would dislike this activity. 5 = I would dislike this activity very much.

Dating Activity	Your Rating	Your Date's Rating	Difference
Going to a school dance			
Relaxing and cruising around in a car			
Attending a musical program			
Eating dinner at a nice restaurant			
Attending a friend's party without parental supervision			
Having a picnic and swimming			
Double-dating with good friends			
Attending a friend's party with parental supervision			
Attending a youth program at your house of worship			
Going to a sports event			

Scoring: For *each* activity, determine the difference between you and your date or friend by subtracting the highest score from the lowest score. Record the results as follows.

Total 0s ____   Total 1s ____   Total 2s ____   Total 3s ____   Total 4s ____

If you have identified *six or more* dating activities with a difference of 0 or 1, you have several similarities and will probably enjoy dating. Discuss with your date the activities you both enjoy and share your reasons for enjoying these activities.

If you have identified *four* or *five* activities with a difference of 0 or 1, your differences are far more numerous than your similarities. You will probably enjoy occasional dates in areas of common interest.

If you have identified *fewer than four* activities with a difference of 0 or 1, your differences are far more numerous than your similarities. It is unlikely that you will enjoy spending a lot of time together.

In all cases, discuss with your date your areas of similarity and differences and why each of you feels the way you do.

Marriage

From the time you were a small child, many of the stories you read probably taught the importance of marriage and living "happily ever after." Read the case study and answer the questions that follow.

Mario Santos and Ashley Pritchard are both seniors at Manchester High School. Mario and Ashley have dated since the tenth grade, and they have been going steady for the past six months. They have even discussed getting married.

Mario will soon complete a tech-prep program in business education. Following graduation, Mario plans to enter a one-year data-processing program at Fairpoint Community College. He presently works part-time and has saved $3,800 for tuition and books. Mario plans to live at home while attending Fairpoint, and his parents have agreed to provide some financial assistance.

Ashley is in a college-preparatory program but has decided that she doesn't want to continue her education after high school. She works part-time and has $4,500 in her savings account. She wants to get married, buy a couple of motorcycles, and travel around the country for a year or two.

Mario thinks they would be better off postponing the wedding until he gets his associate's degree from Fairpoint. However, he is worried that Ashley will break up with him if he doesn't do what she wants.

1. Do you think Mario and Ashley will live "happily ever after" if they get married after they graduate from high school? Explain your answer.

   _____

   _____

2. What responsible behaviors is Ashley demonstrating?

   _____

   _____

3. What irresponsible behaviors is Ashley demonstrating?

   _____

   _____

4. What responsible behaviors is Mario demonstrating?

   _____

   _____

5. What irresponsible behaviors is Mario demonstrating?

   _____

   _____

6. How would you handle this situation if you were Mario?

   _____

   _____

7. How would you handle this situation if you were Ashley?

   _____

   _____

Parenting and Work

Having a child can have a dramatic effect on a couple. One partner might want to drop out of the workforce to care for the family, yet more income will now be needed. On the other hand, both partners might prefer to continue working outside the home. Learning to accommodate the responsibilities and expenses of child care when both parents continue to work outside the home dictates changes in lifestyle as well as marital and family adjustments.

If you become a working parent, with a working spouse, which of the home tasks listed below do you expect to do to help with the responsibility of raising children? Rate each activity using the following scale.

Rating Scale: 1 = Never; 2 = Rarely; 3 = Sometimes; 4 = Frequently; 5 = Always.

Parenting Home Tasks

___ Participating in children's activities	___ Driving children to activities
___ Vacuuming or cleaning floors	___ Bathing the baby
___ Rocking the baby	___ Buying family presents
___ Paying household bills	___ Taking care of sick children
___ Reading to the children	___ Cooking family meals
___ Washing dishes	___ Feeding the baby
___ Maintaining the car	___ Cleaning bathrooms
___ Shopping for groceries	___ Doing household repairs
___ Doing yard work	___ Arranging child care
___ Helping with homework	___ Buying clothing for the children
___ Doing laundry	___ Taking children to the doctor
___ Changing diapers	___ Disciplining children

Total your scores for the Parenting Home Tasks and write that number here. _____

Using your total score, circle the degree of responsibility that you expect to share for the parenting home tasks.

Total Score	Degree of Responsibility
24–48	Little or none
49–72	Less than your spouse
73–96	More than your spouse
97–120	Most or all

1. When both parents work and are tired, how can they still be effective parents and effective employees?

_____

_____

2. If you were the father of a small child, would you prefer that your wife have a career outside the home or be a "stay-at-home" mom? Explain your answer.

_____

_____

3. If you were the mother of a small child, would you prefer to have a career outside the home or be a "stay-at-home" mom? Explain your answer.

_____

_____

4. Do you believe that the father of a child should stay at home and raise the child or be employed? Explain your answer.

_____

_____

5. The labor force participation rate for mothers of children younger than one year old fell by 2.4 percentage points to 53.9 percent in 2003. This rate has fallen almost every year since 1998. Why do you believe this is happening?

_____

_____

6. A major concern for working parents with school-age children is having them come home to an empty house while the parents are still at work. If you didn't stay home alone, what did you do instead? If you were a latchkey child, how did your parents solve the problem? How did you feel about coming home to an empty house?

_____

_____

7. The Family and Medical Leave Act of 1993 ensures millions of employees up to 12 weeks of unpaid leave from their job to deal with a birth, adoption, or medical emergency in the family. Does this law ask too much of employers? Explain your answer.

_____

_____

8. How far should an employer go in helping resolve an employee's conflicts between work and family?

_____

_____

Working Mother magazine annually lists the best companies for working mothers. Using the *Occupational Outlook Handbook (OOH)*, list three careers that would be available in each of the following industries that were on *Working Mother's* most recent list of the top 100 employers.

Insurance companies: _____

_____

Pharmaceuticals companies: _____

_____

Banking companies:_____

_____

Computer/software companies: _____

_____

Telecommunications companies: _____

_____

Chemical companies: _____

_____

Publishing companies: _____

_____

Many parents decide to work out of their home when their children are small. Scan the *OOH* and Chapter 16, and select four careers that lend themselves to "homesite-worksites."

1. _____

2. _____

3. _____

4. _____

What career could you see yourself operating from home? _____

How would you juggle the demands of a crying baby and an impatient customer?

_____

_____

_____

_____

_____

Babysitters' Guide for Working Parents

Prepare an information sheet that busy working parents can give to their child-care providers. It should include the child's complete legal name, nickname, age, emergency telephone numbers, emergency medical information such as allergies or medications taken, and the name and phone number of the closest neighbor or other individual available to assist if needed. Add any other information that you feel is needed. Write the first draft of the guide in the space below.

_____

_____

_____

_____

_____

_____

_____

_____

_____

_____

_____

_____

_____

_____

_____

_____

_____

_____

_____

_____

_____

_____

_____

_____

_____

_____

_____

_____

_____

Who Will Care for Your Child?

For single parents with incomes slightly above or below the poverty level, a lack of child care is a serious obstacle in obtaining and keeping a job. The vast majority of parents in this category has inadequate education, job training, and work experience.

Almost 90 percent of children living with a single parent live with their mothers. As a group, these women often have lower-than-average incomes. As a result, many of the nation's children live in poverty and the consequences of that poverty for many years. Women's career choices often don't pay enough to support a family. Review the occupations listed in the *OOH* and select five jobs that a woman could do that would enable her to support herself and her children and that do not require a four-year college degree. Look particularly at nontraditional careers for women in the trades.

a. _____

b. _____

c. _____

d. _____

e. _____

1. Imagine yourself as a single teenager parent without welfare payments or child-care support. If you accepted a full-time job in one of these occupations, how much money could you expect to earn per day?

_____

2. If you hired a friend or neighbor to baby-sit, what would he or she charge per day? _____

3. What would a professional child-care center charge per day?_____

4. What effect will being a single parent have on your career opportunities?

_____

_____

_____

5. In your opinion, what are the major advantages or disadvantages of being a single parent?

_____

_____

_____

6. In your opinion, what are the major advantages or disadvantages of being the child of a single parent?

_____

_____

_____

7. There are more than 1,000,000 one-parent family groups maintained by men. This is more than a three-fold increase since 1970. Do you believe that fathers can raise their children as well as mothers? Explain your answer.

_____

_____

_____

_____

_____

_____

_____

_____

8. Financial support for children who live apart from their fathers, and the lack of it, is of increasing concern. The Child Support Enforcement Program is an effort to collect child support from parents who are legally obligated to pay. Is this a good idea? Explain your answer.

_____

_____

_____

_____

_____

_____

_____

_____

9. Many high-school-aged mothers do not establish the paternity of their child because the father has no money. However, as the father gets older and starts working, he will be able to support the child and provide benefits such as health care. If paternity is established legally, even if the order for support is delayed, it means that collecting child support will be easier later on. Is this fair? Explain your answer.

_____

_____

_____

_____

_____

_____

_____

_____

Divorce Observations

In the space below, reflect on what you have learned about divorce from friends who have divorced parents. Without using any names or personal references, discuss in writing the pros and cons of getting a divorce. Conclude with your opinions regarding marriage and suggestions that you think would help make a marriage work.

_____

_____

_____

_____

_____

_____

_____

_____

_____

_____

_____

_____

_____

_____

_____

_____

_____

_____

_____

_____

_____

_____

_____

_____

_____

_____

_____

_____

_____

_____

_____

_____

_____

_____

Plan Number Two

Murphy's Law states, "Anything that *can* go wrong *will* go wrong." Most people would disagree with Murphy, but it is true that a good plan doesn't always work. Situations change, and plans must be adjusted. Having a backup plan (plan number two) is always a good idea. Consider the case of Jim Stolz.

Jim is married and has two small children. He is a college graduate with a major in social work. Jim likes to help people solve their problems, but he also enjoys working outdoors. He is considering two job offers.

The first job offer is from the Green Mist Lawn and Tree Service, a locally owned company. After six weeks of training, Jim would be a crew leader in the tree division. The beginning salary is $3,000 per month. During the busy summer season, Jim would be expected to work longer hours and some Saturdays. As a supervisor, he would not be paid overtime.

The second job offer is from a government-funded social agency. Jim would interview elderly clients who are experiencing financial and medical problems. His hours of work would be 8:00 a.m. until 5:00 p.m. Monday through Friday. The beginning salary is $2,900 per month. Jim's opportunity for promotion is very good.

If Jim accepts the job with Green Mist Lawn and Tree Service, he wants to be involved in some type of leisure-time activity helping people. If he accepts the job with the social agency, he wants to be involved in some type of leisure-time activity in the outdoors.

Write a brief plan for Jim that includes the job he should accept, the reason it should be his first choice, and a plan for his leisure-time activities.

_____

_____

_____

_____

Write a backup plan for Jim. Assume that the second job offer is still open.

_____

_____

_____

_____

What adjustments will Jim need to make if plan 1 doesn't work out and he decides to follow plan 2?

_____

_____

_____

_____

Finding the Right Words

Chapter 21 of your textbook contains numerous terms that employers and workers use. Recognizing and understanding these terms will help you make the important career decisions you will soon face.

Fill in the blank spaces in the vocabulary terms to complete the following sentences.

1. _____ is the process of having social engagements with someone you are romantically attracted to.

2. A _____ is a physician who specializes in children's medical care and diseases.

3. When a woman changes her work schedule to accommodate her young child or children, she is said to be on the _____.

4. The _____ provides workers with 12 weeks of unpaid leave from their job to deal with a birth, adoption, or medical emergency in the family.

5. The process of seeking someone's affections is known as _____.

6. _____ is another word for accumulated.

7. When a person is _____, he or she is free from the rule.

8. _____ refers to the time during the workday when parents' thoughts turn to their children who are getting out of school.

9. The parent who does not have primary custody of the child but has a responsibility for financial support is the _____.

10. During the _____ stage of life, most adults establish a unique sense of self that is separate from their original families.

11. _____ is another word for "carefully considered."

12. The _____ stage of life occurs when the working years are over.

13. The _____ stage of life occurs during the working years.

14. Your _____ is the carefully considered involvement of your personal beliefs and behaviors in choosing, training for, performing, and planning your life's work.

15. The ideas and feelings within you that give you a sense of right and wrong make up your _____.

Checking Your Location

For each of the following statements, write **F** if the statement is more false than true. Write **T** if the statement is more true than false.

____ **1.** Lasting relationships begin with people who make you feel lovable and capable.

____ **2.** The kind of love that leads to marriage and family responsibilities affects career roles and goals.

____ **3.** In 51 percent of married-couple families, both the husband and wife work more than 35 hours per week.

____ **4.** Employers use work and family policies as a competitive tool to recruit and keep skilled workers.

____ **5.** In the year 2003, among married-couple families, the proportion in which both parents worked was 73.2 percent.

____ **6.** In today's family structure, fathers accept many responsibilities that women traditionally performed, such as preparing meals, changing diapers, and doing laundry.

____ **7.** The Family and Medical Leave Act of 1993 requires all employers to provide unpaid time off for the birth or adoption of a child.

____ **8.** Children in a single-parent home are more likely to live in poverty than children living with both parents.

____ **9.** Helping your child master the developmental needs of childhood is an important preparation for the child's future career success.

____ **10.** In a single year, approximately one divorce occurs for every two marriages.

____ **11.** Although the characteristics of each person are different, many of the changes that take place during the adult years are predictable.

____ **12.** The responsibility for your friendships, love relationships, and career path is shared with your friends, parents, teachers, and employers.

____ **13.** Realistic expectations can be a source of discouragement and underachievement.

____ **14.** Mature adults remain firm and unchanged in the face of events that are beyond their control.

____ **15.** Learning certain life skills at each stage of your development will help you grow into a mature person and be successful in your chosen career.

On a separate sheet of paper, rewrite the statements you marked false and make them true. Include the number of each statement you write.